Best Seat In The House!

Diary of a Wrigley Field Usher

by
BRUCE BOHRER

ECKHARTZ
PRESS

ISBN: 978-0-9904868

I dedicate this book with love to my son, Jason, in hopes that he will someday witness that day that he, I and millions of others dream about; that he will be able to take his daughter, my darling granddaughter Lucy, and his beautiful wife Stacy to a World Series game at Wrigley Field. Hopefully, I'll still be around so that we can make it a foursome, and we'll see an usher at that game that remembers me and will offer us the Best Seat in the House.

CONTENTS

INTRODUCTION

I've been a Cubs fan, and consequently, a fan of Wrigley Field for over fifty years. For most of those years, I was like most diehards, following the team closely, going to as many games as I could, wallowing in misery every time they disappointed, and relishing the very rare good times. But, in 2003, I took my passion for the team to the next level—I began working as an usher at Wrigley Field—not something I had planned for those fifty years, but as I look back now, a dream come true.

The thought of keeping an account of my experience at Wrigley Field didn't occur to me right away. In fact, I don't think I got the idea until my second year on the job. Consequently, unlike most of this book, the experiences I relate for my first year, 2003, aren't broken down by date. Instead, I relate some general impressions and recollections from that year. My second year, 2004, you'll notice, only has a couple of entries. This is where I recounted my daily routine.

In 2005, I realized it would be cool to have a more extensive record of my experiences as an usher for the Chicago Cubs, so I became more conscientious about writing down things that I experienced while at the park. During most games, I scribbled notes to myself (somewhat surreptitiously, as I didn't want anyone to know what I was doing) to help me remember a particular tidbit or experience. I was fairly diligent about entering the notes on the computer, so as to capture each experience with as much detail as possible.

While typing up an entry in 2005, it occurred to me that my personal journal might be interesting to Wrigley Field fans around the world. My personal journal would become a book. The format of entering specific memories by date began in 2005 and continued through my last day of work, April 21, 2011.

Throughout the book, my goal is to relate the wide variety of experiences that an usher encounters while on the job, from sad to humorous, from maddening to wacky. While reading my stories, you'll notice some recurring themes. For example, there are many entries in which I point out the unsurpassed passion of Cubs fans. There are others in which I note that the Crowd Management supervisory staff is not particularly nurturing. The purpose of my story is not to extol the typical Cubs fan nor is it to be critical of the organization. It is to give you a real sense of what it's like to work as an usher at Wrigley Field.

I hope you enjoy taking the ride with me. Like they used to say on Dragnet… "The stories you're about to read are true. The names have been changed to protect the innocent."

BATTING PRACTICE

March 29, 2003

Today was the first day of a two-day training program
that all new employees of the Cubs Crowd Management staff
are required to attend. The first day is exclusively for new
hires, while the second day is for both new and returning
employees.

I was dressed warmly and a bit nervous on that Saturday
morning, making sure I arrived in plenty of time for my first
session at 10:00. Upon arriving at Wrigley Field, we were
told that the training session would be about three blocks
east in the auditorium of a neighborhood school. Why they
couldn't just tell us to report directly to the school is beyond
me. Although I was early, I quickly discovered that I was by
no means one of the earliest. There were dozens of (mostly
older) individuals sitting in those old fashioned wooden
auditorium chairs.

I took a seat along with my fellow freshmen and waited
with anticipation. We wound up waiting quite a long time,
and the man at the head of the auditorium fidgeted, waiting
for the rest of the inductees to show up. Finally, we began.
He introduced himself and some of the Crowd Management
staff, and then showed us a video of highlights from the
2002 Cubs season. Next, he distributed several forms for us

to complete. One of the forms asked what position within Crowd Control we were interested in. I could choose to be an usher or a crowd control staff member. "What's the difference?" I wondered. Nobody around me seemed to be perplexed by that question, so I put a check mark next to "crowd control" as it paid a bit more and sounded more impressive.

Brief presentations by representatives from a variety of Cubs offices including personnel and payroll were next on the agenda. We also were given instructions on how to complete "incident reports." These are forms that we have to submit whenever something out-of-the-ordinary happens while we're working a game. We were given several handouts including the all-important "Event Operations Handbook", a manual that we were told to read prior to our next training session.

We also were given a schedule of home games. I had been told during my initial interview that crowd control staff members were required to work a minimum of forty-one games. We were instructed to take the schedule home, indicate which games we wanted to work, and bring the completed schedule back to the next training session.

Next we walked to the park to tour the Crowd Management Office and get our locker assignments. We were broken into small groups to take the trek over. During my walk, several of my new colleagues and I introduced ourselves.

"What's the difference between usher and crowd control?" I asked our group leader.

"An usher checks tickets and shows people to their seats," he explained. "Crowd control staff walk the park before, during and after the game to look for potential problems."

"Like what?" I asked.

He described several scenarios including those in which fans are not heeding the directions of an usher, are showing signs of intoxication, become sick, or become engaged in altercations with other fans. There was no way I wanted to deal with angry, vomiting drunks. That wasn't worth the dollar per hour more I would receive as a crowd control. I told him that based on what he just told me, I thought I'd prefer to be an usher rather than a crowd control.

"No problem," he said. "Just tell them when we get to the office."

We arrived at Wrigley, and waited in line to procure a locker. The men's locker room is about the size of a school classroom. We were admitted to the locker room about twenty at a time and told to find a locker and a locker partner. Chaos ensued, as everyone tried to find a partner and the best locker location. Not knowing anyone, I was scanning the room to see who appeared to be as lost as I felt, when Maurice Greenely, a tall, somewhat ragged man with a graying beard asked me if I wanted to share a locker.

"Sure," I said. Maurice became my first buddy at my new job. We shared a locker for the next two years.

April 5, 2003

Part two of training on the subsequent Saturday included lunch because the food service people were being trained that day, and they needed some guinea pigs. We played the role of the customer and were given a hot dog and a coke.

In addition to this blind-leading-the-blind exercise, part two of training consisted of a presentation from an employee of the Bureau of Alcohol Tobacco, and Firearms who spent about fifteen minutes talking about the importance of being aware of bomb threats and what to do when we suspect someone of crowd-threatening behavior. He had his bomb-sniffing dog with him. Fido proceeded to do some show-and-tell for us. All of this was quite frightening. My mind drifted to the terrifying things that I suppose could happen in a place like Wrigley Field. This was less than two years after September 11, so the idea of someone targeting Wrigley was not difficult to imagine.

After lunch, each of us was paired up with a veteran partner for some cursory training. Our partner showed us how to take tickets from fans as they entered the park, the ins and outs of showing fans to their seats, and other very important information, that frankly, should have been given a full day rather than the hour or so that was allotted.

After this, supervisors distributed a take-home exam to test our knowledge of policies and procedures, Cubs history, and those sorts of things from the "Event Operations Handbook." We were told to complete the test and bring it back with us when we report to work on Opening Day.

We finished the day with an evacuation drill—an exercise that illustrated how to lead the crowd in an orderly fashion out of the park in case of emergency. Those uneasy feelings from earlier re-appeared.

"What have I gotten myself into?" I thought. "Would I come out of this job alive?"

It didn't take long, though, for the anxiety to dissipate, as we were quickly excused and told to make sure we got to the park in plenty of time on Opening Day. Opening Day! Now, that's what this was all about. Not bombs and terrorists, but home runs and hotdogs.

THE FIRST INNING—
THE 2003 SEASON

TEAM RECORD: 88-74
STANDING: 1ST PLACE
MANAGER: DUSTY BAKER
ATTENDANCE: 2,962,630

Opening Day! I was as excited about reporting to work
for my first game as an usher at Wrigley Field as I'm sure
any diehard Cubs fan would be before going to his or her
first game. In preparation for that big day, I slept over at my
son Jason's apartment the night before. He had a place that
was walking distance from Wrigley Field, so I figured I'd
take advantage and give myself plenty of extra time to report
to work. The best laid plan: the game was cancelled due to
snow. SNOW! Oh, no! When I called in to see if the game
had been called off, I was told that it was, but if I was willing, I could come in and help shovel the field. This created a
tough decision for me. I'm sure if I volunteered to shovel, I'd
make a good first impression. I guess I wasn't that interested
in first impressions, though—I politely declined; postponing
my personal Opening Day.

First Impressions

For some reason, the very first recollection I have is watching the odd actions of a very disheveled looking fiftyish-year-old man with unkempt hair and a gray scraggly beard. I don't think he was a season ticket holder, but he attended a lot of games that year, and he was always one of the very first fans to arrive. As soon as he got in the park, he'd rush down to the first row of seats by the Cubs bullpen and set himself up to catch batting practice foul balls, big mitt and all. It was an odd scene—dozens of kids were anxiously waiting to catch a ball…and so was this guy. When a ball came near him, he shoved kids out of the way so that he could catch it. The guy probably caught an average of five or six balls per game. I wonder what he did with all of them.

Counting Tickets

I was assigned to take tickets at the entrance gates two or three times that year. After the bulk of the crowd had entered the stadium, we had to count the number of tickets to make sure the number jibed with the number the gate turnstile had recorded. At one particular game, I had been counting tickets at Gate K which is by the left field foul pole. In the fifth inning or so, ushers who took tickets were excused to count their tickets in the boiler room. Yes, the boiler room! It wasn't as hot as you might think it might be, but believe me, it was an eerie feeling as about three of us stood at a table counting tickets in that dark, dingy room. My count turned out to be way off from the turnstile count. The goal was for us to be within ten of the turnstile count; I think I was about forty off. I was told to recount. And so I did. Off by a lot again.

"Oh, no," I thought, "would I be fired so early in my tenure?" Here I was, a fifty-something rookie usher about to be let go because I didn't know how to count. They had me try one more time. Still off. I left the park that day wondering if I'd get a call the next day telling me not to come back. But that call never came. Less surprising....I was never assigned to count tickets again that year.

Making Friends

A much more pleasant memory from that year is of a middle-aged married couple, Harry and Andrea Silverman. The Silvermans were season ticket holders and had been attending Cubs games for many years. I was introduced to them midway through that season by an usher named Sally. Sally and the Silvermans had become good friends over the years and even socialized and vacationed together. Harry was a typical frustrated diehard whose negativity about the team was warranted. Andrea wasn't nearly as invested in the team. I think she came to the games because she was a trooper, devoted to Harry. They were a very nice couple who I saw at most games that I worked. They are representative of the many fans who I got to know and who I miss seeing. Like the two girls from Buffalo Grove High School who I saw a lot my first couple of years. Many of the games that they stopped by to say hi were on days that they should have been at school.

Brushes with Greatness

One day while working the bleachers midway through

the season, I felt a tap on my shoulder. I turned around to see Ryne Sandberg standing in front of me! Taken aback, I said, "Ryne!!!" I guess when you're shocked, you say what comes naturally, and that's what came out. He asked, "Would it be OK if my family and I sit here—my wife wants to get a perspective from the bleachers." I thought to myself, "Ryne Sandberg is asking ME if he can sit here?" I said, "Of course, sit anywhere you want." I felt like adding, "I can shine your shoes while you're watching the game if you'd like." He was extremely nice; he even gave me an autograph for my son. Toward the end of the season, I saw him again, reminded him of our earlier meeting, and asked him to autograph the bill of my cap. He graciously accommodated. He is as genuine as he seems on TV.

One day while working at the stairway that leads to the Press Box, I was anticipating the opportunity to see Shania Twain who was singing "Take Me Out to the Ballgame" during the seventh inning stretch that day. Because I knew she had to walk right past me to get to the WGN-TV booth, I was keeping an eye out for her. Turns out she walked right by me, and I didn't even know it until a colleague pointed out that she had just walked past. So much for old eagle eye! I DID see Baseball Commissioner Bud Selig that day who, unlike most celebrities, did not acknowledge me as he walked by.

Because Wrigley Field is such a mecca, many celebrities attend Cubs games. Other celebrities who have walked past or sat in my section include: Penny Marshall, Vince Vaughn, Bill Murray, Ron Howard, Governor Rod Blagojevich, Senator Dick Durbin, Alex Rodriguez , Mia Hamm and

Robbie Gould. Jesse Jackson has attended many a game. I've also seen John Cusack riding his bike home from the park on several occasions. And naturally, I've seen and talked to many local broadcasters. Most of them are friendly; especially Tom Skilling who talked to me like we were long-lost buddies.

Memorable Events

When the Yankees came to Wrigley Field in 2003, it was the first time they had ever played at Wrigley Field in regular season play. And it was the first time since 1938 when the two teams played in the World Series. So this was a big deal—the two most storied franchises in baseball at America's most storied ballpark. The series was electric; it rivaled any playoff game that I had ever been to, and I'm sure it was just as exciting as any World Series game. The Cubs wound up winning two of the three games, so there was joy and exhilaration in heavy doses that weekend. And what made it even more exciting for the ushers was that Yankee fans tip! We are not accustomed to receiving tips (except when we dry off seats after a rain delay and the occasional fan realizes we've gone beyond the call of duty), but apparently in New York tipping is customary. I say bring back the Yanks.

Perhaps the most memorable game of the Yankees series was the Saturday game in which Roger Clemens pitched against Kerry Wood. The Cubs won the game 5-2, giving Kerry Wood his fiftieth major league win. I was thrilled, as I was a huge Kerry Wood fan and never a big fan of Clemens, although I certainly respect his talent. In the fourth inning, Wood and Hee-Seop Choi collided while going for a pop up.

Choi fell to the ground and was unconscious. An ambulance had to be brought on the field via the gate in right field to take him to the hospital. I can't remember ever seeing that happen before. There was an eerie silence as medical personnel tended to Choi. Fans cheered "Hee-Seop Choi, Hee-Seop Choi", as the ambulance left the field. Needless to say, it was a very scary episode.

One of the most emotional days of my first year was Ron Santo day. It's always exciting when one of your childhood heroes is honored by having his number retired, and Santo was no exception. He holds a very special place in the hearts of so many Cubs fans, not only because of his dedicated years as the Cubs third baseman, but perhaps even more because of the years he so passionately covered the Cubs as their radio color man. The ceremony was extremely emotional—probably because so many aspects of his life were brought to mind: the tragedy of the 1969 season; the fact that he had not been inducted into the Hall of Fame, and his struggle with diabetes. The skies had been gray all morning and threatened rain as the ceremony began. Symbolically and eerily, as Santo stepped up to the microphone behind home plate, the clouds began to part. And just as his jersey was being raised up the left field foul pole, the sun broke through and revealed bright blue skies. You could feel the emotional tingles throughout the stadium.

The Pennant Race

As August rolled into September, the excitement level was at a frenzy as the Cubs were inching toward their first post-season eligibility in five years. The day the Cubs clinched the division, they played a double header, thanks to a prior rain-delay game they had to make up. It was Rosh Hashanah, the Jewish New Year. In observance of the holiday, I had not scheduled myself to work so that I could attend religious services. The Cubs won the first game, guaranteeing them a tie for the title. Winning the second game would have clinched the title, but the second game wasn't scheduled to start until mid-afternoon and I had already returned home from services.

I HAD to be there when they clinched!

So I called the office to see if they would let me come in to work. They said no. I suggested that they could really use me—wouldn't they need extra security to control the crowd if they won? They still said no. I practically begged. Even my good friend Kathy in the office couldn't give me the OK to come down. Very disappointing! Looking back, I understand why they didn't want to let me come in—they probably got lots of similar requests from other ushers. Perhaps I should take solace in the fact that my son (who told me that Wrigley Field is *his* temple and consequently he didn't need to go to services) was at the park that day. At least someone in the family got to be there.

The Media Incident

When the Cubs were the hottest thing in town during the late summer, everyone wanted a piece of the action. A former colleague of mine who worked in the PR department at Harper College (where I worked for thirty years) told me that at the College's previous board meeting, both the *Chicago Tribune* and the suburban *Daily Herald* asked her if

Harper had any Cubs connection. She told them that Bruce Bohrer, the College's recently retired director of admissions, was employed as an usher. As a result, both papers had a reporter call me at home and interview me about my experience and the hoopla that had been taking place the past month or so. Both also said they would send a photographer out to Wrigley to take my picture. On the day of the planned photo shoot, I told the Crowd Management Office that there would be two photographers looking for me, and I told them why.

"Did you get permission to be interviewed?" they asked.

"No," I said. (I had never thought about doing that…why would I?)

They implied I was in big trouble for talking to the media without our boss' permission.

"It'll be a feel-good piece," I pointed out, "and send a positive message about Crowd Control."

After they talked to the boss I was told to call both papers and have them cancel the articles. The *Tribune* agreed not to run the article, but the *Herald* wouldn't accept the idea, and called the Cubs PR people to complain about censoring employees. Ultimately, the *Herald* ran the article and a picture of me in the stands on the front page. Naturally, I heard from lots of people as a result, many of whom I hadn't heard from in years. Once the article was out, the Cubs never mentioned it to me.

The Playoffs

Probably my most vivid memory of 2003 is working game six of the playoff series between the Cubs and the Marlins on October 14th. The Cubs were ahead 3-0 in the eighth inning, and I was sitting at my station, mentally rearranging my personal schedule so that I could be sure that I would be available to work all the World Series games. Yes, I'd have to change a few meetings, but who cares?—I was going to have the chance to work at Wrigley Field to see the Cubs play in the World Series for the first time in almost 100 years! I had to make sure that I was at EVERY game. The rest is history— I think I need not say any more. Besides, it's too painful to think about.

At the end of the year I was nominated for "Rookie of the Year."

I didn't win. But as they say, it's just nice to be nominated.

THE SECOND INNING—
THE 2004 SEASON

```
TEAM RECORD: 89-73
STANDING: 3RD PLACE
MANAGER: DUSTY BAKER
ATTENDANCE: 3,170,154
```

By the time my second season rolled around, I had a regular daily routine on game day.

The Commute

Crowd Control staff are not given parking spaces at Wrigley because the number of spaces is so limited. Management constantly encourages us to take public transportation to the park. Unfortunately, taking public transportation from the suburbs is not very convenient—it would take me a combination of several buses and/or trains to reach the park. That's the main reason I chose to drive.

I live in the northwest suburbs of Chicago, so I typically left home about four hours prior to game time. The majority of games started at 1:20, so I had to be out of the house around 9:15 in the morning. Chicago rush hour is usually over by that time, so bumper to bumper traffic was rare. (The same was true for night and weekend games; start times for these games obviated the need to allow extra time for traffic.) The 45 to 55 minute drive to Clark and Addison got me to the park a bit after 10:00.

Driving home usually took a lot longer than driving to the park. This is because even though I always left the park after the crowd cleared out, much of the traffic was still in the general vicinity. Wrigley stands in the middle of a residential neighborhood. Consequently, the streets around it were not built to handle the huge volume of traffic exiting at one time. Patience was definitely a virtue on the way home.

Parking

Street parking was my only option. Sure, there were plenty of parking lots nearby, but prices ranged from $20 to $50. Spending that kind of money given the salary I was making (as you might have guessed—it was pretty low) would have been out of the question. On a very good day, I'd find a parking space on the street in five minutes or so. Typically, it only took ten to fifteen minutes. Night games were tougher because there were restrictions on street parking in the evening, so available spaces were extremely limited. Weekends were even more difficult--not because of restrictions--but because the mostly twenty-somethings living in Wrigleyville sleep in and don't tend to use their cars until early afternoon. A weekend hunt could take me up to twenty-five minutes and result in a longer walk to the park.

If my pursuit for a parking space was of the shorter variety, I had about a half hour to kill. I filled the time by either reading the morning paper or heading over to McDonald's across the street from the park. Many of the older ushers congregated there prior to the game to socialize and have some breakfast. These interactions provided a great opportunity for ushers to get to know each other better, and I truly enjoyed partaking in them.

Before the Gates Opened

At approximately 10:40, I'd head over to the park in order to arrive in time for our daily pre-game meeting which started at 11:00. I always came to work in uniform. The locker room was just too small to manage getting dressed easily. If the guy with the locker immediately next to mine happened to be at his locker at the same time as me, we'd have to take turns getting things in and out of our lockers. There was no room for two guys to maneuver simultaneously. Consequently, most of us tried to use our time as expeditiously as possible. Go in, get what you needed from your locker, and leave.

The purpose of the pre-game meeting was to give the Crowd Control staff the scoop on what was happening at the park on that particular day and to relate any news that management thought we should be aware of (special groups who would be in attendance, what the giveaway was, team roster changes, etc.). What was not shared with us was news about our colleagues. I'm not talking about trivial information such as so-and-so got a new fifty-inch television. I'm talking about significant events that any staff member would want to know about their colleagues---John is in the hospital, Mary died last week; that kind of stuff. We'd often find out that someone got married or quit weeks after the event. For some reason, management didn't feel it was necessary to share life cycle information with us. Other than that, these were good meetings—short and to the point, occasionally including a joke or two.

The Assignment

At the end of each meeting we were given our assignments for the game. Assignment areas included left field (from home plate to the left field foul pole), right field (from home plate to the right field foul pole), upper deck, bleachers, mezzanine, entrance gates, or (God forbid) a tunnel. Tunnels are the entrances off the concourse which lead to the seats. An assignment there meant I wouldn't be able to watch the game, as the field isn't visible from those vantage points—I'd be spending five hours on my feet watching people buy beer and standing in line for the restroom. Please, God, not a tunnel!

During my first year I had assignments in all of these areas (yes, including the tunnels). This is the case for all relatively new employees and it's a good idea because it gives everyone a chance to see what happens in each area of the park.

I discovered my preferences pretty quickly. Because standing on my feet for more than several minutes has always given me problems, I dreaded assignments that involved standing. The only assignments that didn't involve standing were the lower levels in left field and right field. By the middle of my first year, most of my assignments were in the left or right field areas, so more often than not I didn't have to stand.

On the Job

We were responsible for cleaning the seats in our section with a management-supplied chamois. Because the night crew did a great job of power washing the stadium after the preceding day's game, the seats were usually relatively clean. Sometimes, however, the cleaning crew must have missed certain sections and/or a fan had been particularly messy the day before, and a seat needed a particularly good wiping down. Other times you could tell birds had been around, if you catch my drift.

Once seats were cleaned, it was our job to stand at our station, welcome people with a friendly smile (which was not hard to do, as I was almost always happy to be there), answer questions, give directions, and show people to their seats. The first hour and a half or so was always laid-back, people are always in a casual frame of mind before the game. About a half hour before game time, people started arriving in bigger numbers, and things got a bit more hectic. Often I'd have to multitask, answering one party's question, while showing another party to their seat. Then, about ten minutes prior to game time, fans started showing up in droves, and it was challenging to try and keep on top of everything. By the end of the first inning, things usually quieted down, and most fans were settled in their seats.

Once the crowd was seated and involved in the game, my responsibility was to make sure that only fans who had tickets for my section were allowed access. When I worked the field boxes (the second set of seats above the field), this was usually not a problem, but the club boxes (the lowest set of seats) were a different story. Those seats are SO good, lots of people tried to sneak down to them. (I can remember doing the same thing when I was a kid.)

Many of their explanations about why it was OK for them to sit there were amusing; others were outrageous. Our instructions were to always strive for "seat integrity." In other words "don't let 'em down there if they don't belong there." It's a policy I agree with and one I was good at enforcing (as noted in many of my supervisors' evaluations), but there were times when I disregarded the rules if I felt there was a good reason to do so. For example, after a rain delay when most of the seats in the section were empty, I found it difficult and somewhat ludicrous to tell someone they couldn't sit there.

On most days, I was able to watch the majority of the game. Sure, I had to tend to fans' needs, but usually that took no more than a pitch or two. Frequently I'd be asked to take a picture of a fan or a group. Interestingly, many people wanted to include me in their pictures; I'm not sure why, but my image must be on a lot of fireplace mantels. In any event, I became quite proficient at photography, always suggesting that we include the iconic scoreboard in the background. When I was about to snap the shot, I'd tell the subject(s) to say "Cubs Win!" (unless they were losing badly that particular day). That became my trademark—several other ushers asked me if it was OK if they used it.

Postgame

When a game ended I was either dismissed or, if I had been working a lower box section, I was supposed to go down to the wall by the field and help prevent fans from jumping onto the field. This part of the work day was usually a lot of fun, as all fans were permitted to come down there, and a good percentage of those who did had never been so close to the field and were in awe. Many were tourists who had marveled at the park for the past few hours; they were usually more than anxious to share their exhilaration with a Cubs employee, namely me. I loved talking to these folks about the field, the team, and Chicago. I became a concierge, of sorts, recommending restaurants, and places to see. I also took lots of pictures of fans during this post-game period. On a typical day I took a couple of dozen pictures. Too bad I didn't get paid by the picture.

The Usher Diary

I wanted to give you that insight about my day-to-day life as an usher to help you understand some of the diary entries I make here and in the following chapters. These are my real thoughts as they occurred on the dates mentioned. Just to give you a reference point, I've also included the pitching matchups and the final scores of each game. Maybe you were there too!

April 12, 2004 (Opening Day)

Greg Maddux (Cubs) versus Kris Benson (Pirates)

It was less than forty degrees with a strong wind off the lake today. Just brutal. And the Cubs were just as miserable.

Final Score: Pirates 13—Cubs 2

April 16, 2004

Sergio Mitre (Cubs) versus Aaron Harang (Reds)

Four days later and forty degrees warmer--beautiful day and a fantastic come-from-behind win, as Sosa and Alou hit back-to-back homers in the bottom of the ninth. The crowd didn't want to leave at the end of the game. Sammy Sosa tied Ernie Banks at 512 career homers. This does not please me, as Ernie is my hero and Sammy is not one of my favorites.

I worked Section 25 which is to the right of home plate before the game started today. Most of the ushers who work in this area are veterans, and I was reminded how seriously many of them are about "seat integrity", the concept of making sure that fans don't sneak down to better seats. They really go after people with a vengeance. Once the game started, I was a "break usher" –the usher who relieves other ushers as they take their breaks. This isn't an easy job, as you have to constantly remind yourself what section you're covering. Additionally, you don't get to know the people in your section, so you have to ask everyone to see their tickets. All of them have already shown their tickets to the other usher, so when you ask to see them again, they're often not happy campers.

I saw the white-haired lady who the WGN cameras always show singing "Take Me Out to the Ballgame" during the seventh inning stretch. She met my eyes with a smile. I asked her who she knows at WGN that makes sure she is on TV all the time. She told me nobody—that they just showed her one day and she assumed that because she is at almost every game in her front row seat, they just decided to make a tradition out of it.

Final Score: Cubs 11—Reds 10

April 19, 2004

Matt Clement (Cubs) versus Jimmy Haynes (Reds)

I worked for the first time today as a ticket taker at Gate F which is the main gate on the corner of Clark and Addison. While rubber banding a stack of tickets together, a strong gust of wind came along, and the tickets blew out of my hands. It looked like confetti; you know, the kind we'll see in a parade for the Cubs after they win the World Series. My fellow ushers working nearby helped me retrieve them. They all knew how important it was that I had them in my possession, as my counts need to jibe with the turnstile. When it came time to count later, I was off by eighty; much more than is acceptable. My guess is the supervisor recorded the turnstile number incorrectly. So what did he do? ---he told me to give him three of my stacks of 25 so we would not have to worry about it. Later I was sent to work the bleachers, and was reminded that the amount of beer consumed there on any given day could easily fill half of Lake Michigan. These twenty-somethings who have nothing to do on a Monday afternoon in April get pretty bleary eyed and can barely walk by the end of the game.

Final Score: Cubs 8—Reds 1

In May, the Diamondbacks, Rockies, Giants and Cardinals visited Wrigley. I wasn't yet keeping a regular diary at this point, but I did note that the Cubs were only two and a half games behind the division-leading Reds heading into June.

The Astros and Pirates came to town in June, before it was time for interleague play, and then came a visit from the Oakland A's. At the end of June, the Cubs were three and a half games back—and now the Cardinals led the division.

In July the Cubs swept the White Sox. The season should have ended right then and there, because the Cubs lost nine of their next twelve games against division rivals St. Louis and Milwaukee. By the end of July, the Cubs had fallen to ten and a half games behind the Cardinals, and two games behind San Diego for the wild card spot.

July 30, 2004

Mark Prior (Cubs) versus Eric Milton (Phillies)

Today was the first day I noticed the nylon net that was stretched beneath the upper deck. The netting had been placed there because there have been instances of concrete falling from the upper deck. There had been lots written in the newspapers about the perils of attending a game at Wrigley. I can't imagine that management would endanger the lives of anyone in the park. I'm sure the netting will do the job.

Final Score: Cubs 10—Phillies 7

The home games in August didn't go much better. They were only 6-7 at home in August, but somehow entered September still in the playoff race.

I didn't keep regular diary entries during this period, unfortunately. I only wish I had more entries for the 2004 season…

September 27, 2004

Carlos Zambrano (Cubs) versus Brandon Claussen (Reds)

A young man came up to me prior to the game and asked if I could get him access to lower level box seats, as he wanted to propose to his girlfriend and wanted to do it as close to the field as possible. I arranged that for him, took pictures of him on his knee and of him placing the ring on his girlfriend's finger. He then wanted a picture of me with the happy couple. He said he would mail me copies of the pictures (which he did). Later in the game, I arranged to have them come down to sit in the (much better) club level box seats. They were ecstatic!

Final Score: Cubs 12—Reds 5

With only six games to play, the Cubs were in the lead for the wildcard after this game ended, and they had the easiest remaining schedule of the other teams vying for that slot. The Giants tied them the next day when the Cubs lost to the Reds. The Astros tied the Cubs the following day after the Cubs blew it in the ninth inning (again against the Reds). Both teams finished ahead of the Cubs, who won only one more game.

THE THIRD INNING— THE 2005 SEASON

```
TEAM RECORD: 79-83
STANDING: 4TH PLACE
MANAGER: DUSTY BAKER
ATTENDANCE: 3,099,992
```

April 8, 2005

Kerry Wood (Cubs) versus Chris Capuano (Brewers)

My hero, Ryne Sandberg threw out the opening pitch at today's home opener. Let's hope today's game doesn't portend what will be at Wrigley this season—the Cubs' LaTroy Hawkins gave up the tying run in the ninth, and the Brewers went on to beat the Cubs in twelve innings.

Final Score: Brewers 6—Cubs 3

April 23, 2005

Greg Maddux (Cubs) versus Mark Redman (Pirates)

During our pre-game meeting, the head of stadium operations interrupted our boss and asked if he could say a few words. He had never done this before.

"I just want to tell you what a great job all of you are doing. Occasionally we even get letters from fans who remind us just how important you are to the Wrigley experience. I have one right here," he said, holding a letter in the air.

I immediately thought of the woman who I helped on Opening Day by quieting down some rowdies near her seat-- she said she was going to write a letter to tell the higher ups what a great job I did. I thought, "The letter couldn't be from her, could it?" Sure enough, it was. He read the entire (very lengthy) letter. My fellow ushers let out a big cheer when they heard my name. He called me down, shook my hand and gave me a token of the Cubs' appreciation--$10 worth of Cubs Bucs. Wow!—that'll buy me a hot dog and drink. Seriously, that was very nice of them. I got congratulated from my work buddies for the next few weeks. I was a star!

Final score: Pirates 4—Cubs 3

May 6, 2005

Mark Prior (Cubs) versus Corey Lidle (Phillies)

I witnessed another marriage proposal today. Wrigley must have more proposals per capita than any other place on the planet.

Final Score: Phillies 3—Cubs 2

June 10, 2005

Greg Maddux (Cubs) versus Bronson Arroyo (Red Sox)

Today was the start of the Cubs-Red Sox interleague series. Red Sox fans have so much in common with Cubs fans. Up until very recently, both teams were loveable losers. And Fenway Park in Boston (built in 1912) is so similar to Wrigley (built in 1914). There were tons of fans from Boston in the crowd. They loved Wrigley. I must have had a hundred conversations with them comparing the two stadiums and teams. Most of them agreed that although Fenway and Wrigley are similar, Wrigley is a bit nicer. And they ALL agreed that people from Chicago are a lot friendlier than those from the East Coast. So all in all, one could say that it's better to be a Cubs fan than a Red Sox fan. Oh, wait…the Red Sox have won a couple of pennants recently. Never mind.

Final Score: Cubs 14—Red Sox 6

June 29, 2005

Kerry Wood (Cubs) versus Ben Sheets (Brewers)
One of the fans in my section kept asking if it was OK if he went to the bathroom every time he left his seat. I think he was serious….

Final Score: Cubs 3—Brewers 2

July 1, 2005

Mark Prior (Cubs) versus Livian Hernandez (Nationals)
Sight of the day: a fan in the men's room brushing his teeth.

I was told today that some fans had asked where I was yesterday (I wasn't working.) That's the second time in a couple of weeks that fans were looking for me—I must be quite the usher!

Final Score: Nationals 4—Cubs 3

July 3, 2005

Carlos Zambrano (Cubs) versus Ryan Drese (Nationals)
I worked the stairway at Aisle 16 for the first time today.

Because it is situated between home plate and third base, this is the crème de la crème of stairway assignments. Crowd Control personnel use this stairway to usher VIPs down to the field. Dick, a veteran of about fifteen years is usually assigned this post, but he was on vacation. I'm assuming this assignment reflects the tendency of Penny (my supervisor today) to give me highly desirable posts—she usually puts me at Cross-Aisle 15 which is just to the third base side of home plate and is a favorite assignment of mine. (A cross-aisle is a barrier that prevents people from walking in front of the people sitting in the first row of the field boxes. Working the cross-aisle means telling people they can't walk through a section of seats and have to walk up the stairs and around. You can imagine how much that pisses people off.)

Anyway, working Stairway 16 requires guarding the gate that VIPs use to enter the field prior to the game. The job requires that the usher work with Crowd Control to determine who is eligible to access the field. Today's celebrities included Ron Santo Jr. and Mia Hamm who was singing the seventh inning stretch.

Unfortunately, once the game commenced, I had to stand at the top of the stairs and keep the area clear. This was the first time since my rookie year I had to stand for so long. Fortunately, though, it wasn't too bad despite the fact that the game went twelve innings.

Final Score: Nationals 5—Cubs 4

July 14, 2005

Mark Prior (Cubs) versus Mark Redman (Pirates)
Harry Silverman related a funny story to me. In 1945,

when he was a boy, his father got tickets to a Cubs World Series game. He didn't take Harry and told him, "I'll take you next time."

Still waiting.

Country star Kurt Anderson stopped to pose for pictures and sign autographs for fans. More often than not, celebrities are whisked away to get out of the crowd. It was so refreshing to see a well-known figure demonstrating kindness toward his admirers.

An elderly woman said something to me in a strong British accent. Jokingly, I said, "You're not from Alabama, are you?" She replied that she had just flown in from England to see her grandson, Cubs outfielder Matt Murton, play in his first game at Wrigley Field. Never know who you're going to be talking to.

Another wedding proposal took place today. A young man told me he had arranged with Pete, the head of stadium operations, over the phone to propose to his girl friend near the field. I told him I didn't know where Pete was, but worst case scenario, that if he couldn't find him, he should come down to see me after the game, and I would be glad to video the proposal right by the wall. They showed up after the game, and Pete had them wait until pretty much everybody cleared out. Then Pete showed them to the Cubs dugout. I followed them and captured the proposal on video.

I received my biggest tip ever: $10 from a guy who sat in Aisle 14 Row 11, Seat 1. As he handed me the money, he said, "Thanks for taking care of us." And I don't even think he believes that I did anything special.

Final Score: Cubs 5—Pirates 1

July 17, 2005

Carlos Zambrano (Cubs) versus Kip Wells (Pirates)

I spent much of the pre-game talking to the mother of today's honorary batboy. How thrilled was she? Probably more than her son.

Final Score: Cubs 8—Pirates 2

July 25, 2005

Rich Hill (Cubs) versus Jason Schmidt (Giants)

In the process of changing my clothes in the locker room today, I laid my shirt on top of one of the lockers. When I grabbed the shirt, I noticed that it was covered with dust. I don't think they've dusted there since the Cubs last won the World Series.

Final Score: Cubs 3—Giants 2

Jeremy Burnitz hit a sacrifice fly in the bottom of the ninth to win it.

July 27, 2005

Carlos Zambrano (Cubs) versus Brett Tomko (Giants)

For the first time, I worked with my locker partner Maurice Greenley today. Maurice is quite a character. He started using a cane this year, so apparently he has some rather serious health issues. Nevertheless, he must do an OK job, as he's been with the Cubs for a number of years.

Today the Cubs sponsored a T-ball program for little kids. Kids from various park districts got the opportunity to play T-ball on the field. Very cute. Lots of parents were in my section taking videos of their kids.

One of the beer vendors whispered to me that it was a

slow beer day.

"This whole year has been slow," he added. "Ever since people have been able to purchase tickets online, the crowds are filled with farmers, truckers, and hillbillies, and those people don't drink beer."

Really?

Final score: Cubs 4—Giants 3

Jeremy Burnitz RBI single in the bottom of the ninth to win it.

July 29, 2005

Mark Prior (Cubs) versus Javier Vasquez (Diamondbacks)

I saw a kid with a "no lights" t-shirt today. These shirts were very popular in the 1980s. Many traditionalists (including yours truly) did not want night games to be played at Wrigley, and a rather vocal effort to ban them was quite active. A group called CUBS (Citizens United for Baseball in Sunshine) promoted the concept that baseball was meant to be played in the sunshine. The fan with the shirt told me he got it at one of the souvenir stores across the street. I'm a bit surprised they still make those—nice to know that the sentiment still exists, even though the lights have been here now since 1988.

Section 140 consists of the box seats in the right field corner. There's a group of ushers who always work together there, and have their own "system" in terms of taking breaks, carrying out responsibilities, etc. It was fun to work with them there today, but I was reminded that it's sometimes tough to do things your own way, when a "system" is already in place.

Final Score: Cubs 4—Diamondbacks 3
Cubs score twice in the bottom of the ninth (singles by Michael Barrett and Aramis Ramirez) to win it.

August 8, 2005

Jerome Williams (Cubs) versus Brandon Claussen (Reds)

Got my first "ABCDE" (Above and Beyond the Call of Duty and Expectations) card today. These cards are awarded to Crowd Management personnel who have done something exceptional (according to their supervisor). I got my card from Penny who was surprised when I told her it was my first one. According to the Cubs "Event Operations Handbook," the cards can be redeemed for five "Positive Employee Performance Program Points" and are worth $5 in Cubs Cash. Oh, boy! It was truly nice of Penny to give me the card. She is, far and away, my favorite supervisor.

Final Score: Reds 9—Cubs 4

August 10, 2005

Rich Hill (Cubs) versus Eric Milton (Reds)

When I signed in today, I bumped into Penny, and she asked me what my favorite assignment was on the right field side. It's the first time a supervisor has asked me that, and I'm sure it is a very rare occurrence. Normally supervisors just assign ushers wherever they deem best.

The Cubs, although not officially eliminated from the pennant race, are pretty much out of it. They've been playing miserable, embarrassing baseball the past couple of weeks. I always wondered whether I would still like this job when the team was playing games that didn't matter. So far, the answer is yes. I still love talking to the people who come from all over the world to see Wrigley, and I still enjoy the relationships I have with my fellow ushers. Stay tuned.

Final Score: Reds 8—Cubs 2

August 12, 2005

Carlos Zambrano (Cubs) versus Jason Marquis (Cardinals)

As soon as the gates were opened, a man and his ten-year-old son arrived in the park. Dad found their seats, got settled, and yelled loud enough to be heard all the way in the bleachers, "Hellooo, Wrigley Field."

He was so thrilled to be at the park.

Today's game was against the Cardinals. One fan I see from time to time must have a million different articles of Cubs clothing in his wardrobe. He's wearing something different every time I see him. Today's outfit included a hat with a dead cardinal perched on top of it. Very amusing.

One of my favorite colleagues is Agnes, who must be about seventy-five years old. She stands around four foot eight, has very thin gray hair, is missing a few teeth, and is always wearing a jacket no matter how hot it is, because she is always cold. Many of her verbal expressions are straight out of the seventies. Nothing's quite as funny as seeing her lead the fans in a rendition of "YMCA" when it's played.

Speaking of dancing, the Cubs have a Dixieland jazz band that plays between innings every game. The usher who is working the aisle closest to the band is responsible for keeping fans from walking in front of them. As I was doing so today, a girl grabbed me and started dancing with me to the music.

We were quite a hit.

Around the sixth inning I noticed sports radio host Tom Shaer had taken a seat in my section. I was pretty sure he didn't have a ticket for the seat, so I approached him about it. I had decided that if he played the celebrity card, I was going to insist he move, but if he was a nice guy, I wouldn't. He was sitting with a married couple. When I approached them, Tom said they didn't have tickets for the seats (in fact, I think he said they only had SRO tickets), and that they would gladly move. He was very pleasant and definitely did not pull the celebrity card. I told him to keep his seat.

Final Score: Cubs 4—Cardinals 1

August 14, 2005

Mark Prior (Cubs) versus Matt Morris (Cardinals)

I was assigned to Aisle 104 which is in the left field corner. Of course, I was asked about the Bartman seat. For those who have been living in a cave since 2003, Steve Bartman is the guy who was accused (in my opinion, unjustly) of blowing the Cubs' lead in the sixth game of the 2003 playoffs by reaching over the wall for a foul ball. I used to know his exact seat, but have since (as a defense mechanism, I'm sure) forgotten it. Now I can honestly say "I don't know" when I'm asked.

Somewhere around the seventh inning, I asked a fan who was standing in the aisle to take his seat. He said he would in a minute, but that the guy next to him was "passing gas" incessantly. Other fans in the area chimed in that the guy was drunk and had been farting for a while, but they didn't want to say anything.

What is an usher to do? ---there's nothing in the handbook that addresses this situation. I grabbed Darlene in
crowd control and apprised her of the situation. She was
sort of stymied as to what to do as well. It kept getting worse
until finally, a friend of the guy took him out of the park.
Darlene wasn't quite sure what she should write on her incident report.

Final Score: Cubs 5—Cardinals 4

August 22, 2005

Kerry Wood (Cubs) versus Tim Hudson (Braves)

A sign of our times—a guy caught a foul ball while talking on his cell phone.

I came close to experiencing the first confrontation in
my usher career today. The Cubs were rallying in the ninth
inning, and a fan and his buddy were pretty inebriated. They
were standing up and were very rowdy. I asked them to sit
down, and one of them started arguing with me.

"You're the kind of person who takes the fun out of being a Cubs fan," he said to me. I started to retort (probably
not the wise thing to do, according to the Crowd Control
Handbook and common sense), but just then the game
ended and everyone was out of there anyway. Crisis averted.

Final Score: Braves 4—Cubs 2

August 24, 2005

Mark Prior (Cubs) versus Jorge Sosa (Braves)

A fan mentioned to me that he's been to seventeen Cubs
games in his life and that the Cubs have won every one of

them. He was at the Don Cardwell no-hitter (May 15, 1960) and recalled the game with amazing detail.

His streak ended today.

Final Score: Braves 3—Cubs 1

August 26, 2005

Glendon Rusch (Cubs) versus Jason Vargas (Marlins)

Before the game today, I was talking to twins (brother and sister) who were there to celebrate their birthday. They said their mother used to take them to Cubs games on their birthday when they were kids, so they thought this would be a good way to celebrate. They were hoping to get autographs from Billy Williams and Ron Santo, The brother had 8x10 photos of Williams, Santo, and Banks, and the sister had a copy of Santo's "This Old Cub" DVD.

Shortly after speaking with them, I went to the bathroom and noticed that Santo was signing autographs in the concourse. I rushed back to get the twins and sent them running. They found me later to let me know that the brother got an autograph on his 8x10 of Santo. The sister was not so lucky, but they were both thrilled.

One fan called me a "ticket Nazi" today. Guess management would say I'm doing a good job.

Final Score: Marlins 7—Cubs 5

August 28, 2005

Carlos Zambrano (Cubs) versus Josh Beckett (Marlins)

What a great day! Today was Ryne Sandberg day—the day they retired his jersey and raised it on the right field flagpole. Because I was at Aisle 16, most of the participants in the Sandberg festivities had to walk down my aisle to access the field. This included Sandberg's wife and daughter, Bobbie Dernier, Dennis Fitzsimmons, (chairman of the *Chicago Tribune)* and the chairman of the Baseball Hall of Fame.

I shared short verbal niceties with all of them. It was touching to see some of these big shots relate to the "little people." Fitzsimmons, for example, copied down the mailing address of a woman who wanted Ryne's autograph on a t-shirt she brought along. He promised he would send it to her. A bit later, I let him know that his barber was in the stands with his family and wanted to say hello. He immediately came up to greet them, and even gave the kid a baseball. The Hall of Fame CEO stopped on his way up after the ceremony to talk to a kid too. How Americana!

The ceremony itself was moving. Lots of people (including me) were wiping away tears as Sandberg and others spoke. Appropriately, it was a beautiful day, and the Cubs went on to win big.

Final Score: Cubs 14—Marlins 3

August 31, 2005

Glendon Rusch (Cubs) versus Derek Lowe (Dodgers)

An elderly gentleman in my section related to me that he attended one of the 1945 World Series games. He said he was waiting in line to try and buy a ticket the day of the game and somehow got pushed into a group that was able to get tickets. The seat was in the bleachers, and it cost two dollars.

In the "a bit bizarre" category--I talked to two different guys today who both flew in from New York City--just to come to Wrigley. Both of them had been to Chicago many times before, but had never been to Wrigley, and were a little embarrassed that they had never experienced it. One took the opportunity to accompany his wife, who was here on business. The other just took the day off to fly in for two days and see an exhibit at the Field Museum and enjoy a Cubs game.

A relatively young man from Las Vegas was sitting in Row 2 of my section. When I asked to see his tickets, he took a hundred dollar bill from his pocket and flashed it in front of my face, all while carrying on a conversation on his cell phone. I refused the bribe (stupidly??) and made him leave. I noticed later that he had returned to the same seat. I contacted Crowd Control who escorted him out.

Final Score: Dodgers 7—Cubs 0

September 12, 2005

Greg Maddux (Cubs) versus Aaron Harang (Reds)

I talked to two guys today who had driven from Vancouver to Memphis to see Graceland (every other word out of their mouth was "eh?"). They decided on their drive back home that it would be cool to see Wrigley Field, so they just showed up and got seats that morning. They asked me if they would be able to talk to Ryan Dempster, who is also from Vancouver. It turns out that their seats were right by the bullpen, so they managed to talk to Dempster for a long time.

About forty-five minutes after I met them, another guy asked a question and mentioned he was from Canada.

"Where in Canada?" I asked.

"Vancouver," he responded.

I introduced him to the other guys. Small world, eh?

A woman in the stands looked forlorn. I asked her if I could help her, and she told me she was dying for a chocolate chip cookie. I told her we had none, but that we had chocolate ice cream. That didn't cut it. I offered to go up to the skybox suites, as I was sure they'd have some on the desert tray. I was hoping she would turn my offer down, as I wasn't sure I could do this. Fortunately, she did.

Final Score: Reds 5—Cubs 2

Willy Mo Pena hit a three homer in the ninth (off Sergio Mitre) to win it for the Reds.

September 15, 2005

Mark Prior (Cubs) versus Jeff Suppan (Cardinals)

Sight seen: The first base umpire handing a ball to a dad in the stands who was holding his infant son. Nice! (Although I found out after the game that he knew the family.)

The Cardinals clinched the Central Division here today. There were a lot of Cardinals fans on hand to relish the moment. After the game ended, they did not want to leave. We had to assure them that the Cardinals weren't coming out of the dugout to accept their accolades and had to literally shoo them out of the park. A difficult reminder of what could have been had the Cubs played up to their potential.

Final Score: Cardinals 6—Cubs 1

September 22, 2005

Greg Maddux (Cubs) versus Rick Helling (Brewers)

A group of my friends and I went to a Cubs/Brewers game at Miller Park in Milwaukee today. I noticed an usher or two prior to the game, as well as some usher-types handing out giveaways at the gates, but didn't see any ushers once the game started. I did see some crowd-control types by the dugouts after the game, but that was it. It would be interesting to find out what it's like being an usher at other major league stadiums.

On a similar note, one of my Wrigley colleagues recently wrote the following poem, entitled "The Best" about being an usher for the Cubs:

What makes an employee stand out from the rest?
How can an employee be labeled the best?
It's timing and smiles
It's laughter and pain
It's thirst and it's hunger
It's wet feet in rain
It's friendship and caring
It's helping and leading
It's cleaning and wiping
It's freezing and piping (hot)
It's loving the ivy
It's talking and chatter
It's saying and meaning
"12 innings won't matter"
And maybe the Cubbies have found that by fall,
They ought to just label "the best" as us all.
Final Score: Cubs 3—Brewers 0

September 23, 2005

Glendon Rusch (Cubs) versus Wandy Rodriguez (Astros)
I worked the visitors' family section at today's Cubs/

Houston game. The area was filled with reporters from Texas TV stations. They were there to interview Houston families about the hurricane about to hit the Gulf Coast. The mother of one of the Houston players was taking quite a few pictures and asked me to grab Agnes for a picture. She remembered that last year Agnes gave one of her grandkids a coloring book and said that Agnes is her favorite usher in all the major league parks.

Final Score: Cubs 5—Astros 4

September 25, 2005

Jerome Williams (Cubs) versus Andy Pettitte (Astros)

Vendors who sell peanuts often toss the bag to the fan. Sometimes it's a rather distant throw. Today one vendor hit a young kid in the face. Fortunately, the kid wasn't hurt. It was rather amusing, though.

I worked with one of this year's rookie ushers for the first time. She mentioned that she wished she had written down all of her experiences at Wrigley. I didn't tell her about my project. Later, as I was writing down a note to myself about the peanut vendor, she asked what I was writing. I told her I was making a reminder to myself to do something later. Didn't want to give away my secret.

Final Score: Cubs 3—Astros 2

September 28, 2005

Mark Prior (Cubs) versus Paul Maholm (Pirates)

Today was the last home game of the season. Appropriately, it rained during much of the game. Even more appropriately, the Cubs had the bases loaded with nobody out in the bottom of the ninth and didn't score. Sums up the season.

Over three million fans came to Wrigley this year. I'm not sure, but I think when PA announcer Wayne Messmer announced this to the crowd, he mistakenly said three million dollars rather than three million fans. How Freudian.

My favorite supervisor, Penny, was named supervisor of the year. Well deserved.

Toward the end of the game a twenty-something who obviously had indulged in a few too many adult beverages tried to get past me.

"My dad has my seats; please let me through," he said.

"You mean your dad has your tickets?" I asked him.

"Oh, yeah," he said, "That's what I meant."

I talked to an elderly gentleman today who was reminiscing about the days before rooftop seats were sold by corporate entrepreneurs.

"One day I knocked on the door of one of the buildings," he said, "and asked if I could go up on the roof. The owner said OK and showed me to a ladder. I climbed right up there and watched the game."

I was talking to Vern, my colleague who calls me Yogi, as he thinks I resemble Yogi Berra (I'm not sure where he gets that from.) He was telling me that for three years he worked the supplemental scoreboards (the ones in left and right field). He said it was a great gig. I asked him why he didn't do it any more, and he told me that the job used to be in the Crowd Control department, but was reorganized into another department for political reasons.

"But you know what?" he said. "I'm probably one of the

only people in the world that took a piss with the Governor. The restroom in the press box area is very small. One day the governor was up there and had to use the facilities. Normally, a bodyguard would go in with him, but because of the space limitations, the governor went in alone. I was already in there doing my thing. We had a nice conversation while we peed."

Final Score: Pirates 3—Cubs 2

At the end of the day the Cubs were nineteen and a half games behind the division leading Cardinals, and ten games behind the wildcard Houston Astros.

October 6, 2005

Today was the end of the season party Free food and drink; the one time a year that the *Tribune* does something really nice for us. It's always fun talking to my colleagues outside of the work environment—most of them are so nice. It confirms how special they are. Dusty Baker (and son) and Gary Matthews were both there. (I didn't see Andy McPhail, who I know was there last year.) Dusty was very friendly and seemed jovial, despite the disappointing season. He shook lots of hands (including mine) and told us how vital we were to the team. I would love to have told him a few things about what I think of his management skills, but we all know where that would have gotten me.

THE FOURTH INNING—
THE 2006 SEASON

TEAM RECORD: 66-96
STANDING: 6TH PLACE
MANAGER: DUSTY BAKER
ATTENDANCE: 3,123,215

February 6, 2006

Sad news—one of my favorite colleagues, Agnes, passed away this month at the age of seventy-four. I'll miss her very much.

April 1, 2006

Today was the annual "veterans train the new employees day." It didn't surprise me that during today's formal program, no mention was made of Agnes's passing. They just don't think like that. Toward the end of the day, one usher asked about it, and the boss mentioned that we will miss her.

They did add a nice twist to the training today—they did a "get to know your colleague" exercise, consisting of a list of questions that we asked our fellow ushers about personal things such as whether they have ever been to a World Series

61

game, or whether they are a Vietnam vet. I wonder what prompted this attempt to add such a humanistic component to our training. I did learn a couple of interesting things about some ushers that I don't know very well. One woman lives in Hawaii during the off-season. Another has seven kids—two sets of twins and a set of triplets!

It was great to see all my old buddies again. I was reminded that I do this in large part now because of the nice people with whom I work. I'm looking forward to Opening Day this Friday.

There are several new supervisors this year. To become a supervisor, one must have worked in the Crowd Control Department for at least a couple of years. The new supervisors know much about most of us and our history of where we've been deployed, so I'm looking forward to some positive ramifications of the personnel changes. Ralph, pretty much everybody's favorite supervisor was there today, but he announced that he will not be returning this year. He has decided to move down to Mexico where he and his wife own a farm. We'll all miss him a lot.

April 7, 2006

Greg Maddux (Cubs) versus Jeff Suppan (Cardinals)

Opening Day this year brought new enhancements to the park—the expanded Bud Light Bleachers (ugh—advertising is beginning to become more acceptable at the one major league stadium that heretofore had banned any ads in the park), the new "Batter's Eye Lounge", the Bleacher Boxes in right field, more restrooms, etc. I have to give credit to the higher-ups here—they accomplished their goal of adding seats without detracting from the intimacy of the park.

Opening Day also brought cold winds. I guess I've learned over the years—I wore seven layers of clothes, and consequently wasn't nearly as cold as I've been in past Aprils. I also took a tip from a friend of mine and wrapped my feet in aluminum foil. That, accompanied by two pair of socks kept my feet plenty warm. However, I had to take one pair of socks off mid-game, as my insulated feet were so covered up that they were getting numb. Upon removing the socks, I discovered that aluminum foil breaks into little pieces as time goes on. I left quite a mess when I attempted to get rid of it in the locker room after the game. Oh, and I wound up with blisters on both feet.

I received my favorite assignment for this important game--Cross-Aisle 15. As a result, I worked with my pal Oliver. He told me HBO contacted him a couple of weeks ago about including him and his fellow usher and wife, Louise in a special they're doing on Wrigley. Of course, he had to refer them to the office to get permission. Hopefully, they'll grant it—it would be cool to see them on national television.

Oliver also mentioned that he has multiple myeloma. They've been experimenting with various drugs. He seemed as upbeat as possible about it. He's the best.

For years, the Cubs have reserved specific (and very good) seats for the team doctors. This year they decided to experiment with the seating assignment -moving them from their traditional Aisle 123 to guess-where?? Cross-Aisle 15. I talked quite a bit today with the team physician and the team orthopedic doctor. Both are very nice guys. I hope they decide to keep them there. It would be nice to buddy up with them, assuming (and hoping) I'm at that post a lot this year.

On the field, the Cubs played a terrific ball game—great pitching, fielding and timely hitting.

Final Score: Cubs 5—Cardinals 1.

April 11, 2006

Glendon Rusch (Cubs) versus Bronson Arroyo (Reds)

Harry Silverman joked with me that he asked the Boss' right hand man to assign me to the section that they sit in so I could watch over them.

Final Score: Reds 9—Cubs 2

April 26, 2006

Angel Guzman (Cubs) versus Scott Olsen (Marlins)

I worked Section 101 today with Maurice Greenley (my old locker partner). Section 101 is now the "family section" (having been relocated there this year from the left field bleachers.) The previous family section was truly that—an area where alcohol was not permitted. In this "new" family section, fans may drink beer, but they cannot purchase it from a vendor if they are on the right side of the aisle. They either have to go to a concession stand or they can purchase it from a vendor on the *left* side of 101.

Sound of the game--a fan who spoke with a Hispanic accent yelling to the Marlins' blonde-haired and blue-eyed left fielder who made a nice catch off the Cubs' Matt Murton: "Go back to your own country."

One of the fans in my section today was Joe Girardi's high school football coach. Joe was a quarterback on his team at a high school in Peoria. The guy visited with Girardi yesterday and mentioned that Joe is a great guy.

Final Score: Marlins 7—Cubs 5

April 30, 2006

Carlos Zambrano (Cubs) versus Chris Capuano (Brewers)

Rain delayed the start of the game. During the delay, I saw Cubs closer Ryan Dempster come out of the dugout and into the stands. I'd never seen a player do that. He started to walk up toward the press box. I assumed he was going there to do an interview, thinking that it was strange he was going via the stands. He got up to the grandstand, took a seat and started signing autographs. He stayed there for close to an hour, signing one after another. How refreshing to see a player remember what baseball is supposed to be all about! I asked Oliver if in all his years he had ever seen a player do that, and as expected, he replied in the negative.

Final Score: Brewers 9—Cubs 0

May 12, 2006

Angel Guzman (Cubs) versus Woody Williams (Padres)

Early in the game, I observed two young guys hanging by the stairway. I approached them and asked them where their seats were. They pointed to seats in my section.

"We're just going to wait here by the stairs until the inning is over," one of them explained. "We don't want to make anyone miss part of the game while we climb over them to get to our seats."

"It's OK," I said. "You can go to your seats now."

They did, and on the very next pitch one of the two guys caught a foul ball on the fly. Talk about timing!

Final Score: Padres 10—Cubs 5

May 14, 2006
Rich Hill (Cubs) versus Clay Hensley (Padres)
Sound of the game--one of the vendors was screaming "Mother's Day gifts!" as he hawked beer today.
Final Score: Padres 9—Cubs 0

May 17, 2006
Sean Marshall (Cubs) versus Zach Day (Nationals)
Tonight's game was held up by rain and hail. It was quite a sight to see fairly large pellets falling on the field. Even more spectacular was the rainbow that gleamed over the scoreboard. Natural beauty behind a man-made wonder.

One woman got very angry with me when I questioned about her ticket. She was indignant that I should do such a thing.

"I've been a season ticket holder for ten years," she said.

"Sorry, but I don't know you," I explained.

Upon leaving the game, she came up to me and planted a kiss on my cheek.

"Now you know me," she said.
Final Score: Cubs 5—Nationals 0

May 18, 2006
Kerry Wood (Cubs) versus Ramon Ortiz (Nationals)
It happened again—my magic touch. A father with his little girl asked if he could move down a few rows so they could still be in the sun. (We were in Aisle 12 where the sun gradually moves up the rows as the afternoon goes on.) I

told him OK. The next inning a foul ball came his way; it was deflected off a fan right into his lap. I should start advertising the power I have in attracting the prized Rawlings.

Dick mentioned that he thought our boss was displaying a kinder, gentler side this year. Can't say I disagree. They gave us Snoopy stuffed animals (nothing's as cute as Snoopy wearing a Cubs uniform) leftovers from a recent giveaway day. Maybe they ARE starting to be a bit more employee-friendly.

Oliver is in the hospital with kidney problems. That, coupled with the skin cancer he's facing worries me. I'm hoping for the best.

Final Score: Nationals 5—Cubs 3

May 26, 2006

Carlos Zambrano (Cubs) versus Tim Hudson (Braves)

Sight seen--a squirrel running through the stands. Here's hoping it'll reverse the curse of the goat. So far, no go, as the Cubs lost again. They continue to play miserable baseball. The fans have begun booing a lot—can't blame them. It's going to be a long year.

Final Score: Braves 6—Cubs 5

The Braves scored three runs in the ninth against Cubs closer Ryan Dempster to win it.

May 28, 2006

Jae Kuk Ryu (Cubs) versus John Smoltz (Braves)

It was in the nineties today—first really hot day of the season. I worked Aisle 122 and had a lot of people who had tickets in the lower boxes wanting to move up to the fiel-

boxes where the sun doesn't shine. I listened to a lot of "my mother can't take the heat" and "I don't want my child in the sun" type situations. It was musical chairs all day. I tried to accommodate people as much as possible.

I noticed a pompous guy I've seen several times before sitting in the first row of my section. I knew I didn't seat him there, so I asked Vern if he had seen the guy's ticket. He told me this guy is the number one *Tribune* stockholder, so we let him sit wherever he wants.

Celebrations today included another marriage proposal and a guy enjoying his thirtieth birthday.

Sound of the game—a fan who made several trips with his kids to the concession stands remarked to me on his last trip downstairs, "The tickets were the cheapest part of my day."

A bit of excitement on the field today as a fan ran out on the field from the seats by the right field bullpen. Needless to day, he was apprehended immediately by crowd control, much to the chagrin of the crowd.

Final Score: Braves 13—Cubs 12

May 29, 2006

Kerry Wood (Cubs) versus Elizardo Ramirez (Reds)

As part of the Memorial Day celebration, a moment of silence was held at about 3:00. Kind of an eerie feeling. There were 40,000 people and you could hear a pin drop. Although, if you listened carefully, you could hear the raucousness of the rooftop fans who either didn't know about the tribute, or didn't care.

It was very hot again today. I have to credit management—they are very good about giving us plenty of water and sunscreen on hot days. About the seventh inning, it started to rain. We were so heated up, that the raindrops were uncomfortably cold.

Sight seen—a girl whose shirt said "Cubs Virgin." I asked her exactly what that meant, and she explained it was her first Cubs game. I told her that's what I thought, but just wanted to be sure. That got a laugh from the fans nearby.

Final Score: Cubs 7—Reds 3

May 31, 2006

Carlos Zambrano (Cubs) versus Eric Milton (Reds)

I discovered that my fellow usher Byron's home is not too far away from mine. He was so excited to learn that. He mentioned that his wife was buried at Shalom Cemetery, so I asked if he was Jewish. He replied in the affirmative, and we proceeded to play a bit of Jewish Geography. He grew up about a mile from where I did and went to Senn High School, which is where I would have gone had my family not moved to a new home.

Byron introduced me to the umpire locker room manager's wife. I've seen and talked to her before without knowing who she was. She is quite a character; always dressed in outlandish Cubs clothing, including hat, earrings, bracelets and more.

Sound of the game-- A woman returning to her seat was having trouble finding it. I recognized her and called her over. She thanked me and then remarked, "I didn't recognize any of the bald spots down there."

I talked to two guys who bicycled from New York City to

Chicago this week. It took them almost three weeks to do so. Their goal: to see Notre Dame and Wrigley. They were tired, but excited after having made it to the park.

My supervisor today was Vic. He informed me that he was putting a positive evaluation in my file. I was shocked—not so much because no supervisor has ever told me that he/she was going to do that, but because it came from Vic, who is very quiet and rarely starts a conversation. In any event, it was a nice testament. I did read the comments he made—something about how dependable I am, etc. —but I was so shocked it didn't really sink in.

Final Score: Reds 3—Cubs 2

June 14, 2006

Greg Maddux (Cubs) versus Roy Oswalt (Astros)

I talked at length with a fellow usher named Peggy today. Although we have known each other since I started and have joked around a lot (she is always laughing and seems to have a great time), we never had that get-to-know-you conversation. Turns out she is a Chaplin in a hospital not too far from where I live. (Our conversation began because she told me she recently treated a patient who knows me—but she can't remember her name.) She has two masters degrees—one in Theology and one in Guidance and Counseling. We shared information about our career histories.

I also had a fairly long conversation with a young usher who, I believe, started the same year I did. I'm guessing she's around nineteen. She mentioned that she was going to buy a new $600 cell phone for only $450.

"That's still a lot of money," I said.

"I know," she replied, "but it has a lot of cool features."

I doubt that she comes from much money; she mumbled something about her whole salary going towards this. She reflects her generation pretty well---immediate gratification is paramount.

Another usher named Suzette came up to me in the eighth inning to ask if she could borrow a few bucks. This woman has always struck me as a bit odd; nevertheless, I gave her five dollars. She said she'd return it next time we work together.

It drizzled before game time, and so I wiped down seats as I sat patrons, like we always do when seats are wet. I started to dry the seat of one guy who told me quite adamantly that he didn't want me to do that. Got to wonder why—I guess it takes all kinds.

Pre-game Flag Day ceremonies included parachutists who landed at second base. I never realized how high up those guys start out; it seemed to take fifteen minutes for them to land. Their precision was astonishing.

A first time visitor from San Francisco told me how excited he was to finally be here.

"I've watched the games on WGN for fifty years," he said. "I even remember watching games in black and white. I can still see Ernie Banks standing right over there at shortstop."

This guy is representative of the millions who, even though they didn't grow up in Chicago, were able to watch Cubs games on WGN-TV. People from all fifty states have fond childhood memories of coming home from school and tuning in the Cubs playing day games at beautiful Wrigley Field. Because the Cubs were the only major league ball club to play day games, those games were often the only ones kids could watch. It was so easy to get hooked on the Cubs playing in the sunshine. Forever optimistic Jack Brickhouse kept us believing that maybe this would be the year.

These days WGN televises significantly fewer games. I know times have changed, and we're in the age of cable TV and big television contracts, but I think in the long-run, the Cubs will lament the fact that it's harder to find the Cubs on free national television. Over the years, that great national base of fans will diminish, resulting in a lot less people coming to Wrigley because they didn't have the opportunity to follow the team.

Overheard while waiting in line for the bathroom from a guy who obviously was impatient---"Hell, I think I'll just pee in my pants."

One teenage girl asked me if she could run down to take a picture. I told her yes, and while she was gone, I asked her friends if they knew what she wanted to photograph.

"Michael Barrett's ass," they replied.

Final Score: Astros 5—Cubs 4

June 15, 2006

Carlos Zambrano (Cubs) versus Fernando Nieve (Astros)

I spoke to a gentleman from Nashville today who came to the game with his father and four year old son. It was his son's first game. His father mentioned that the kid has a large artwork of Wrigley in his room and he was very excited to see the real thing.

This reminded me of the day I brought my son to his first Cubs game. He was three and a half years old. I remember hoping he would make it through four or five innings. To my delight, he lasted the whole game, mesmerized by the sights and sounds of the place. I asked him not too long ago if he remembers that game. He replied that he doesn't, which doesn't surprise me. I don't remember my first game either. So many fans have told me that they remember their first game. Really?

Final Score: Astros 3—Cubs 2

June 17, 2006

Carlos Marmol (Cubs) versus Justin Verlander (Tigers)

I was offered a $100 bribe today from a Tigers fan in town from Michigan. He told me he gives his regular usher at Comerica Park in Detroit $100, and the guy lets him sit in good seats. I told him it doesn't work that way here.

A Tigers scout who I met a few weeks ago was sitting in my section prior to the game. At one point he asked me to watch his bag while he went on the field. Lots of thoughts ran through my head about what I could find if I went through the bag… perhaps all kinds of dope on different teams. I could really be a hero, huh?

As the Cubs fell to fourteen games below .500, a beer vendor was coming up with some doozies to match the crowd's mood. His creative sales pitch yells included "pain-killers" and "the beers are cold as the Cubs."

Final Score: Tigers 9—Cubs 3

June 26, 2006

Greg Maddux (Cubs) versus Chris Capuano (Brewers)

As I was going to sign out today, I bumped into Suzette. I

reminded her that she owed me five dollars. She told me she was just laid off because she had left her post for five minutes. She didn't offer to return the money, but said she'd see me later this week. How is she going to see me if she was just laid off? I'm a fool.

Final Score: Brewers 6—Cubs 0

June 28, 2006

Carlos Marmol (Cubs) versus David Bush (Brewers)

Michael Barrett, the Cubs catcher who is finishing up a ten-game suspension spoke to us at our pre-game meeting today. I guess he has a lot of time on his hands. I'm not sure what the impetus was for the little rah-rah session, but he told us how much the players appreciate all we do. He also told us not to get too discouraged, despite the fact that the Cubs are twenty games under .500. He seemed rather upbeat considering how miserable the team is this year. I guess when you get paid those big bucks, it really doesn't matter how good your team is doing.

I saw Suzette again today. (Guess she wasn't laid off, after all!) I asked her for my money again. She said she gets paid at her other job this Friday and will pay me after that. I asked Charlene, another usher if she knew Suzette and told her why I was curious. She replied that not only did she know her but she also loaned her money a couple of years ago (she said it was more than five dollars), and never got the money back. I WILL continue to request the money.

Jane came rushing up to me saying she smelled cigar smoke…like a detective trying to chase down a criminal. She needs to get a life.

Final Score: Cubs 6—Brewers 3

June 30, 2006

Sean Marshall (Cubs) versus Jon Garland (White Sox)

Over the years, I've seen a lot of fans who don't respect the National Anthem, but today I saw a guy who took the cake. While the anthem was being sung, he was talking on his cell phone to someone in the upper deck, and waving in a very animated fashion. In the sixties and seventies I wouldn't take my hat off during the anthem as a protest to the government and what it stood for during the Vietnam War. But, I never would have demonstrated the kind of disrespect this fan did.

After the game, a fan came up and asked me a question I've never been asked before. "What is the dirt on the pitcher's mound composed of and why is it watered down after the game?"

Who do they think I am, Madam Curie?

Final Score: White Sox 6—Cubs 2

July 2, 2006

Carlos Zambrano (Cubs) versus Mark Buehrle (White Sox)

I worked by the visitors' (White Sox) bullpen today. The bullpen catcher (last name of Lee) represents what baseball should be about. Prior to the game, he was signing autographs, giving baseballs to kids, posing for pictures, and joking around with the fans. It was interesting how he only interacted with kids and women (mostly attractive women, at that).

Today's marketing sales pitch from the beer vendor who uses clever lines to sell his beer: "Sunday brunch, get your cold Sunday brunch."

Today marked the end of the "cross town rivalry" series. The Cubs won today, after dropping the first two of the series. This marked the first time that the Sox have played at Wrigley as World Champs, which was hard enough to take, but the Cubs are also currently one of the three worst teams in baseball. The crowds over the weekend were about fifty-fifty in terms of which team they rooted for. I have to admit the Sox fans didn't rub it in our faces as much as I thought they might.

While working the game, today I reflected back to the Cubs rivalry in my own family. Although my mom was a Cubs fan, my dad was a dedicated White Sox guy. In fact, when they were kids on the West Side of Chicago, my dad and his twin brother made the bold decision to switch loyalties from the Cubs to the White Sox. The story goes that in those days EVERYONE in Chicago loved the Cubs, and the Sox were the city's poor stepchild. Harold and Ira decided they wanted to be different and so they hooked on to the Sox. They used to tell me about the fights they got into because nobody, but nobody liked the Sox. I chose the Cubs over the Sox because the word "Cubs" just sounded better than "Sox" to me. Now, there's a good reason for choosing a team.

Final Score: Cubs 15—White Sox 11

The Cubs scored seven in the first inning, and then held on to win.

July 14, 2006

Greg Maddux (Cubs) versus Steve Trachsel (Mets)

Today's game was delayed by a downpour in the sixth inning. I've never seen it rain so hard at Wrigley. I had to guard the first base dugout during the storm—the water was well above my pants cuff. My socks were soaked for the rest of the game.

In downtown Chicago last week, I bumped into one of the younger ushers at a play. She had always struck me as a bright girl; motivated and responsible. I mentioned that I hadn't seen her around this year. Turns out she had worked a few games less than the minimum last year because of school, and was told she'd have to reapply for a position. They told her to choose—school or the Cubs. Fortunately for her, she chose school and is now working at the Drury Lane Theater as an usher.

Final Score: Mets 6—Cubs 3

July 16, 2006

Sean Marshall (Cubs) vs. Orlando Hernandez (Mets)

I finally got my five dollars back from Suzette today. She better never ask to borrow money again.

I was talking to Louise about how the park is always full, despite the pathetic season the Cubs are having. She told me that after the major league strike of 1994, many fans were very perturbed about the situation and were slow to return when a settlement was finally reached.

"Some of the ushers were asked to make phone calls to season ticket holders to plead with them to return to the park," she said.

Boy, things have changed.

Cubs blew a 5-0 lead today against the Mets. Although I've given up caring whether they win or lose this season, there's still something rotten about losing to the Mets. There can't be a Cubs fan on the planet who doesn't recall the summer of 1969, when the Cubs were in first place all season until September. They proceeded to blow a nine game lead to the Mets. Today's loss hurt even more because there were so many Mets fans in the stands.

Most bizarre incident of the day: When the national anthem was announced, a fan who was holding two beers asked me to remove his cap and hold it for him during the song.

Final Score: Mets 13—Cubs 7

July 19, 2006

Greg Maddux (Cubs) versus Roger Clemens (Astros)

As I showed a couple to their seats, they made me think twice.

"We'll get you on the way back," the man said. I must have looked perplexed, so he clarified. "I want to give you a tip, but I only have a twenty."

"Twenty would do just fine," I joked.

They never did "get me on the way back."

I worked Aisle 7 today by the Cubs bullpen. This game featured Greg Maddux against Roger Clemens in what could very possibly be the last time two 300-game winners would face each other. I had to monitor a lot of people who wanted a picture of Maddux as he warmed up. I felt a strange sense of power that I don't think I've felt before as I determined who could go down for a picture and for how long.

A couple of fans had some of their belongings on the wall. I asked them to remove their things, because we don't want things falling on the field. Tim (a crowd control guy, who is very nice) called me over to tell me that he thought the rules have changed.

"Before the game starts," he said, "fans CAN keep stuff on the wall."

"That's news to me," I said.

"I just heard it a few days ago," he replied.

The next day I asked a couple of colleagues, both ushers and crowd control, if they were aware of this change. Nobody was. They never tell us about these things.

I think I must have reached a milestone as an usher. I had three different fans come up to me to say hello, as they recognized me from prior games. I guess I can consider myself a seasoned veteran now.

The well-publicized game featuring the two masters of pitching wasn't exactly a classic. Clemens outperformed Maddux. The Cubs could only muster three hits against him in six innings. Maddux didn't pitch poorly, giving up three runs on seven hits in seven innings.

Final Score: Astros 4—Cubs 2

July 20, 2006

Carlos Zambrano (Cubs) versus Andy Pettitte (Astros)
A record day--two $5 tips.
Final Score: Cubs 4—Astros 1

July 28, 2006

Carlos Marmol (Cubs) versus Jason Marquis (Cardinals)

Another good tip day; I got a twenty dollar tip from who else?—a New York Yankees fan.

Sight seen—Ryan Dempster cooling down bleacher fans with a garden hose during batting practice on this ninety-plus degree day.

I worked with Luellen, one of the two ninety-plus year olds at Aisle 17 (it's her permanent assignment). I think I've worked with her once or twice before. She has a reputation of being very difficult to work with, but I didn't have any problems. In fact, at the end of the game, she even told me she enjoyed working with me.

Before the game started, I noticed a sixty-something-year-old guy flirting with Luellen. Go figure. She told me he comes around every so often, and she can't stand his advances.

There were two girls sitting in our section who had obviously had some work done. They were extremely attractive and anxious to show it all off.

Sight I noticed for the first time, but it's been going on for years–pigeons scavenging the bleachers as soon as the crowd leaves.

Final Score: Cubs 6—Cardinals 5

July 30, 2006

Carlos Zambrano (Cubs) versus Chris Carpenter (Cardinals)

Spent some time watching fellow usher Hillary today. She records which seats are taken so she can keep track of exactly who's not supposed to be in her section. She gets my vote for most conscientious usher.

Final Score: Cubs 6—Cardinals 3

July 31, 2006

Mark Prior (Cubs) versus Brandon Webb (Diamondbacks)

Our guest speaker at today's meeting was Gary Pressy, the Cubs organist. He mentioned during his talk that the Cubs are one of a very few teams that still have an organ.

I worked Aisle 6 today. A fan vomited in the tunnel leading to my aisle. (Irv, clean up in Aisle 6!) It's not the first time I've seen a fan get sick, and I'm sure it won't be the last.

Sight seen- Ryan Dempster reaching over the bullpen wall and giving candy bars to a couple of fans during the game.

I talked to a fan who said she came to the game tonight to celebrate the fact that she has contracted with an attorney to file for divorce after sixteen years of marriage. She was ecstatic. I also talked to a couple of kids today from Germany. They are here with their friend who lives in Chicago. I tried to impress them with what I remembered from my high school German. Impressed, they were not.

Final Score: Diamondbacks 15—Cubs 4

August 2, 2006

A fan from New Jersey told me today that she's been a diehard Cubs fan all her life. Says she got hooked when she worked at a bar in her home town where they always had the game going on WGN.

Today's game was rained out. Many people were very

disappointed, because they had come from out of state (I lost count of how many states.)

August 4, 2006

Carlos Zambrano (Cubs) versus Tom Gorzelanny (Pirates)
During batting practice a foul ball was hit in my area. A seven-year-old kid was running after it. I picked it up and handed it to him. He was ecstatic, jumping for joy. Gave me a real high. Later, his mom took a picture of him, me, and the ball.
Final Score: Pirates 6—Cubs 0

August 5, 2006

Mark Prior (Cubs) versus Zach Duke (Pirates)
I rode to work today with Mike Terson, who is now the Cubs weekend PA announcer. I know Mike from my Harper College days. We recently bumped into each other at the Buffalo Grove Park District where he now works, and he offered to drive me in on days we both work. He has a sticker for the employee parking lot. It will be nice not to have to search for a street parking space on weekends.

Mike and I talked about our respective jobs. I mentioned that I have always been very impressed with the rapidity with which the scoreboard operator gets the balls and strikes on the board. He told me that the guy who runs those controls has written cues about each umpire and their idiosyncratic movements as they call strikes. This helps him get a quick read on each call.

They had free ice cream for us at our pre-game meeting; which was a first. Nothing was said as to why, but I'm guessing it was their way of thanking us for working during this very hot eleven game home stand (longest of the season.)

Sight seen- Connie's pizzas being delivered by a Connie's employee to a group of fans. I hadn't realized that this could be arranged.

Two very obese guys approached me in about the fifth inning. One of them claimed to be a Chicago cop. He showed me his badge, but who knows if it was the real thing. They asked me if they could move down to my section because the two seats they had were too small for them, and they noticed there were several four-sets available in my section. I wanted to oblige them, but knew that because they were so big, they would block the view of fans behind them. I agreed to let them sit in the top row of my section.

Not long after, a fan a few rows below them mentioned that my police friends were using vulgar language. I immediately asked them to leave. They did so, but as they left, the one with the badge shook my hand and whispered in my ear, "I hope you die in your sleep."

Very nice.

Final Score: Cubs 7—Pirates 5

August 6, 2006

Rich Hill (Cubs) versus Ian Snell (Pirates)

The administrative staff took a group photo of all the ushers at our pre-game meeting today. I have no idea why.

I worked Aisle 101 today. I asked if we were still treating the left side of that aisle as the family section. Nobody, including Penelope, my supervisor knew. I said that I would just use my judgment, which was agreeable with Penelope.

For the first time that I'm aware of, fans did the Wave today. In the past I've seen feeble attempts at a wave, but it never really worked. Today, it was a success despite a few boos from the crowd. Tradition mandates that we just don't do the Wave at Wrigley.

Final Score: Cubs 6—Pirates 1

August 18, 2006

Carlos Marmol (Cubs) versus Jason Marquis (Cardinals)

Sight seen--kid with a Mohawk hairdo. I haven't seen one of those in a while. I accidentally bumped into him—the guy must use a ton of mousse to keep it erect.

Today's giveaway was hosted by a food promotion company. They were giving away all kinds of free food—cereal boxes, granola bars, and Breyer's ice cream bars. Ushers were invited to partake. They must have brought 50,000 ice cream bars—they were giving them away at Gate F as well as tossing them to fans in the stands. I think I had four of them, myself. They were quite tasty.

Final Score: Cardinals 11—Cubs 3

August 20, 2006

Juan Mateo (Cubs) versus Chris Carpenter (Cardinals)

Today was the Chicago Air and Water Show. The crowd was treated to incredible demonstrations in the sky over the park. It was definitely more entertaining than what was taking place on the field, as the Cubs lost another one.

Stephanie, an usher who worked with us up until a couple of years ago, was sitting in my section today. I've seen her at quite a few games this year which doesn't surprise me, as she is a huge Cubs fan. I wonder how often I'll go to games once I've resigned.

Final Score: Cardinals 5—Cubs 3

August 21, 2006
Rich Hill (Cubs) versus Jon Lieber (Phillies)

When I got to my area today, I noticed a ball sitting there—it apparently had been hit there during batting practice. Needless to say, I put the ball in my pocket and waited to give it to a kid who I thought would idolize me for the rest of his life. After carefully scoping out the early arriving crowd, I went up to a five-year-old boy and offered him the ball.

"No, thank you," he said very politely.

I couldn't believe my ears—who would turn something like this down? Shows what a good judge of character I must be. His father, sitting next to him urged him to take it, but he would hear nothing of it. I wound up giving it to the dad, and later saw the kid playing with it.

Also during batting practice-- a thirteen-year-old was hit by a foul ball. Cubs relief pitcher Will Ohman found out about it and gave a ball to the kid. Nice.

Still more BP activity. A guy with a camera asked if he could go down to the wall. He wanted to take pictures of Phillies pitcher Chris Coste. Coste had spent twelve years in the minors, before finally making it up to the Show this year. He wrote a book about his tribulations in the minors and the guy with the camera was the editor of the book. We had a nice conversation. After he walked away, I realized---what a wasted opportunity! I should have gotten some info from him in preparation for my book.

But, lo and behold, as I was leaving the ballpark, there he was again. I couldn't believe it. I told him I knew someone writing a book about baseball (didn't want to disclose that it was me). He gave me his card and said I should definitely have that guy get in touch with him. Maybe this project is meant to be.

Final Score: Phillies 6—Cubs 5

August 24, 2006

Carlos Zambrano (Cubs) versus Cole Hamels (Phillies)

I talked to a guy before the game today who has just completed producing a film about the Cubs' futile search for a championship. It's called *Chasing October...A Fan's Crusade.* Although he's had some financial support from Budweiser and others, he's still looking for a major studio to distribute it. He invited me to the world premiere at the Music Box Theatre next week. I hope to go.

I was talking to some fans from Boston today who told me something I had never heard…that Bill Buckner was injured in that game he made the infamous error with the Red Sox. The guy said the Red Sox manager should never have left Buckner in the game. Buckner has always been one of my favorite Cubs; I hope the story is true, as it sure would make Buckner's ability to cope much easier.

A ploy that failed? A fan tapped me on my shoulder to tell me that I sure looked familiar. I never saw the guy in my life. I have a feeling that he was in cahoots with two other guys who, when I turned around to look, were suddenly sitting in my section. I asked to see their tickets, and sure enough, they didn't have any.

Final Score: Cubs 11—Phillies 2

September 1, 2006

Rich Hill (Cubs) versus Noah Lowry (Giants)

The San Francisco Giants were in town today for the first time this season. Much ado was made about Barry Bonds—the one player everybody loves to hate (including Yours Truly). We were advised during our pre-game meeting to be vigilant for inappropriate anti-Bonds signs and to be especially vigilant when he came out to bat or take the field. So what happened?....he wasn't in the lineup!

Once again today, a fan I had let stay in my section (instead of asking him to move to his correct seat) caught a foul ball.

Final Score: Cubs 6—Giants 2

September 3, 2006

Angel Guzman (Cubs) versus Jason Schmidt (Giants)

Well, today Barry Bonds was in the lineup. I worked Aisle 6 in left field, so I got to experience the full effect Bonds has on the crowd. I learned that he has a bodyguard who sits in the stands along with an undercover Chicago cop.

I worked with Lenore today. She joked that with the city of Chicago debating the "big box store" issue (the city is considering imposing a minimum wage of ten dollars an hour for employees who work in "big box" stores such as Wal-Mart and Target), perhaps they should include those of us who work in big circles.

"Get it?" she said, "Big box, big circle."
Final Score: Giants 7—Cubs 4

September 4, 2006

Carlos Zambrano (Cubs) versus Paul Maholm (Pirates)

I worked Aisle 117 today—the Cubs family section. Although I've worked the visiting team family section many times, I've never worked the Cubs'. It was cool to watch these fans cheer on their husbands, fathers, and sons. Henry Blanco's kids paid close attention when Dad came up to bat. I could see the tension in David Aardsma's father's face while his son was pitching —made me reflect back to when my son was pitching in little league—how nervous I was when he was on the mound. Bob Howry's dad, on the other hand, seemed to take everything in stride, laughing the whole game, even while his kid was pitching.

I was drying off seats when a group of ten-year-old kids showed up with seats in the first row of the field boxes. They had gotten tickets from one of the Pirate pitchers. I had finished wiping their seats down and was about to leave when one of them got my attention.

"You missed a spot," he said. He was serious. Pretty funny.

I found out today that Jay, my locker partner, is proficient in five languages and has taught ESL in several countries including Vietnam and Thailand. He'd like to do that again upon retirement in a couple of years.

Quote of the day—a fan asked if Kerry Wood was pitching today. (He's been on the disabled list for most of the year.)

Shirt of the day seen on a Pirate fan---"Cellar Series 2006".

The injuries on the team continue to mount. Today, Carlos Zambrano, the ace of the staff was taken out in the second inning with back spasms. Upon his leaving the mound, I ran down the stairs past my cousin Ken who has season tickets in Aisle 117 and yelled to him that I was going in to relieve. Could I do any worse than anybody else they've tried?

Fans from Pittsburgh told me today that they are season ticket holders in Pittsburgh and that one of the ushers has been working there since 1936 when he was sixteen. What a journal he could write!

Final Score: Cubs 5—Pirates 4

September 7, 2006

Sean Marshall (Cubs) versus Shawn Chacon (Pirates)

Found out today that Suzette is apparently still asking other ushers for money. One of those ushers is in the process of compiling a list of people she's scammed. I'm not sure what she's planning on doing with the list.

Today's announced crowd of 21,000+ is the smallest they've had since I began working four years ago. It's certainly understandable considering the way the team's been playing. Now that kids are back in school and tourists are gone, it will be small crowds from here on out. One fan was not shy about hiding his feelings,

"I hope you get paid for this," he said.

I met a six-month-old fan today. Her parents introduced her as Addison Kerry. Now, those are diehards!

Sight of the day—Esther, the ninety-three year old usher dancing around to the sounds of "How Bizarre."

Final Score: Pirates 7--Cubs 5

September 13, 2006

Angel Guzman (Cubs) versus Brad Penny (Dodgers)

Worked Aisle 8 today by the Cubs' bullpen. I realized working that area makes me feel like a zookeeper...the players are the animals, and the fans are just gawking at them, or trying to get their attention. There's been more than one instance when I probably should have told a fan to "be nice to the animals."

Talked to a guy who told me he's been coming to games since 1958 and he still has every scorecard from every game.

"They must be worth a lot," his wife said.

"No they aren't," he said. "Because I'll never sell them."

I have scorecards going back to the eighties. I know I always bought scorecards as a kid, but I guess I threw them away when I got home. I wish I kept all those earlier ones. It would have been a lot of fun to relive games from all those years ago.

Talked to someone from Lost Nation, Iowa; population 400. He and his family drove in today to see the game. He said he's been a Cubs fan all of his life and was so excited to be taking his son to his first Cubs game.

While I was in the bathroom today, a fan dropped his cell phone into the trough. Several fans yelled out, "pisser phone". I think he left it there.

I saw Oliver today. He hasn't been working lately due to his poor health. He came to pick up his wife, Louise after the game. He looked quite good, considering.

Final Score: Dodgers 6—Cubs 0

September 15, 2006

Juan Mateo (Cubs) versus Bronson Arroyo (Reds)

Saw another wedding engagement take place today. A young man proposed to his girlfriend in the walkway, between innings. Needless to say, the crowd around him cheered when the girl said yes. She cried and jumped up and down with excitement.

Talked to a guy who had been brought to the park by his wife to celebrate his seventieth birthday. It was his first time at Wrigley. The wife had arranged for their daughter and son-in-law to fly in from New York and surprise him at the ballpark. Very heartwarming.

Final Score: Reds 4—Cubs 0

September 17, 2006

Carlos Zambrano (Cubs) versus Eric Milton (Reds)

Today, local celebrities Antonio Mora of Channel 2 News and one of the *Walter E. Smithe Furniture* brothers were in my section. Both were greeted by representatives of the Cubs marketing department—they wanted to be sure the celebs were having a good time. The marketing reps had gift bags for each of them.

Final Score: Cubs 11—Reds 3

September 29, 2006

Carlos Zambrano (Cubs) versus Josh Fogg (Rockies)

A young twenty-something fan in my section today was

acting more like he was thirteen. He was very persistent (to the point of being annoying) about going down to the first row to get autographs and/or a ball. I tried to be accommodating, and let him run down once in a while before the game and even between innings during the game. His method paid off. He got a baseball and an autograph from Kerry Wood.

Meanwhile, an eleven-year-old boy who had just completed over forty radiation treatments for a brain tumor that had been removed during the summer was also sitting in my section. He and his family were from downstate Illinois and had never been to a Cubs game. The family, of course, was in seventh heaven. The youngster also got a baseball and an autograph.

Early in the game I noticed that a number of manila envelopes were being passed around in the stands. It turns out the envelope contained signs that read "Bring Back Maddux." A note on the front of the envelope asked fans to take one and hold them up during the seventh inning stretch. Lots of fans took one, but the plan failed—I didn't see any fans holding them up during the stretch.

Final Score: Rockies 5—Cubs 2

September 30, 2006

Juan Mateo (Cubs) versus Jeff Francis (Rockies)
Quote of the day from a fan on his cell phone: "I just bought my last beer of the year at Wrigley."

Just like last year's season closer, today's game was such a fitting ending to a horrible year on the field. The game began under beautiful skies and ended with a rain delay in the ninth when the skies opened up. The Cubs had just tied the game 9-9 in the bottom of the ninth and had a runner on base when they called the game. The game resumed about a half hour later, and went fourteen innings.

It was a bittersweet day. It's certainly good to have this miserable season end, and as usual, I am tired of the drives to and from the park, but I have really grown to love the job itself. I enjoy the people I work with so much. I also love talking to the fans at the park. In the past, I wasn't one hundred percent sure if I'd want to return. This year I know for a fact it's something I'll want to do again next year.

Final Score: Rockies 11—Cubs 9

October 1, 2006

Although I didn't work today, the last game of the season, it was a big day in Cubs history. Immediately after the game, Cubs president Andy McPhail announced that he was resigning, a very unexpected event. John McDonough, VP of Marketing was appointed Interim President. Upon hearing that, I immediately recalled that I saw John at the game on Friday. John has always been very friendly, always saying hello when he passed me. On Friday; however, he didn't—I remember thinking he seemed quite preoccupied as I walked past. Now I know why.

As a fan, I was left with a sense of futility upon hearing of McPhail's resignation. I remember being quite excited twelve years ago when they hired him. He brought so much promise to the team--they finally had a guy who could create champions out of the Cubs. Now, twelve years later he was leaving without pulling it off. If he couldn't do it, I'm not sure anyone can….there's something to this Curse thing.

October 5, 2006

Today was the end-of–the-season-party. It was a lot of fun talking to my colleagues. Penny asked if I was planning on returning next year. I said yes, and told her my concern about the possibility of not being invited back because I didn't work forty-eight games this year. She told me the worst case scenario would be that I would receive the "although your performance last year was less than ideal, we still want you back" letter. Stay tuned.

THE FIFTH INNING–
THE 2007 SEASON

```
TEAM RECORD: 85-77
STANDING: 1ST PLACE
MANAGER: LOU PINIELLA
ATTENDANCE: 3,252,462
```

January 19, 2007

I worked the Cubs convention today. While observing Cubs fans who attend the annual event today, I was amazed at some of these "Cubs Crazies" who are so passionate about their team. They walk around sporting Cubs pajamas, Cubs earrings, Cubs license plates; you name it. They bring their autograph books and wait in line for hours on end to get signatures of even mediocre Cubs of the past. I worked the autograph table where former Cubs Ron Coomer and Doug Glanville were sitting. You would have thought they were Ernie Banks and Babe Ruth—we had to cut the line off so that Coomer and Glanville could get to their next gig.

I worked the day with Dick. He informed me that Oliver passed away in November. I was so saddened to hear this news. I talked with Louise, Oliver's wife, and expressed my condolences. I'm pissed off that I wasn't informed about it so that I could have attended the funeral, but the Cubs still don't have any official means of communicating with us about these types of things. Dick also mentioned that he attended the Ushers Union breakfast in December. I asked him how he had found about it, and he said he got an email from Sally. You'd think the Union would invite all members—word of mouth is ridiculous. I would really like to quit the Union, but we all know that will never happen.

It was good to see all my buds at the Convention. Everyone's anxious for the season to start.

April 7, 2007

Today was part two of this year's training. We sat outside in what everybody agreed was the coldest training day ever. The temperature didn't rise above thirty degrees as we remained outdoors for over three hours. Today's session included the usual procedural reviews, including emergency evacuation procedures, and a free hot dog.

There was a bit of discussion regarding the sale of the *Tribune* that was announced earlier this week. Our boss stated that nobody really knows what effect this will have on any of us. No reason not to believe him. This development, though, should provide lots of fodder as the year progresses.

Oliver's wife, Louise told me that Oliver's ashes were spread on the field at the bottom of Aisle 15—where he always worked. How appropriate. Louise seems to be handling his absence quite well.

To their credit, management attempted to abbreviate the program due to the cold.

April 9, 2007

Ted Lilly (Cubs) versus Woody Williams (Astros)

Opening Day. Nothing particularly exciting happened today, considering it was, indeed, Opening Day.

Senator Dick Durbin was in the crowd today. I saw him upon his arrival and then again later when I took a break. He was in the cattle herd going into the men's room. It was interesting that none of the (mostly drunk) fans struck up a conversation with him. Then again, neither did I when I wound up standing next to him at the trough. What, exactly, DO you say to your senator when you are taking a leak?

Final Score: Astros 5—Cubs 3

April 17, 2007

Wade Miller (Cubs) versus Greg Maddux (Padres)

What started out as a beautiful spring day (about sixty degrees at our 11:00 meeting) turned out to be brutal, both weather-wise and game-wise. Around 1:00 the wind started gusting in off the lake, and the temperature dropped about twenty degrees. It would have been bearable (I had my five layers on), but the game went fourteen innings. Of course, the Cubs lost the game. There was one highlight, however. Felix Pie, the much ballhooed center fielder, was brought up from the minors to start his first major league game. He made a spectacular throw to the plate to cut down what would have been the winning run. The throw was the talk of the crowd and of all the sports talk shows later that day.

Final Score: Padres 4—Cubs 3

April 20, 2007

Ted Lilly (Cubs) versus Brandon Looper (Cardinals)

Found out that Mary in the Front Office is leaving at the end of the month. There was a notice about that in *Game Times*, the crowd management newsletter. She's been with the Cubs for eighteen years, and at the age of eighty decided it was time to move on. She's very nice and will be missed. I hope they're planning on doing something for her other than mentioning her in the employee newsletter. Wonder who they'll replace her with—has to be someone else named Mary. Every office MUST have a Mary!

I saw John McDonough today and chatted with him for a bit. He continues to be very friendly and approachable, even after his promotion to president.

I worked with Helene today. Helene is about eighty and is always cold…even when it's not, she's wearing gloves. We were discussing how cold it was the other day. She mentioned that she told Deena, the supervisor that she had a bad headache from the cold and would like to leave. (It was already 5:00 at the time.) Deena told her to "deal with it."

Cody and a couple of the other young guys from the marketing department were sitting around me before the game. Gary Pressy, the organist was pounding out a song, and Cody asked me if I knew what it was. I told him *"Spanish Eyes."* "Oh, that's right," Cody answered. I'm surprised he had heard it before. We went on to discuss how Gary doesn't play the hippest music (much of the stuff he plays is from the 40s, 50s and 60s). Cody said it's probably because Gary wants the opposing team to become sleepy during their batting practice.

Final Score: Cardinals 2—Cubs 1

April 22, 2007

Wade Miller (Cubs) versus Adam Wainwright (Cardinals)

Sound of the game from the beer vendor who always has an amusing pitch: "Beer here. Have LaRussa's drink of choice." (He was referring to the fact that Tony LaRussa, the Cardinals' manager was arrested last winter for DUI.)

Final Score: Cardinals 12—Cubs 9

Albert Pujols hit a three run homer in the tenth inning off Ryan Dempster to win it.

May 4, 2007

Carlos Zambrano (Cubs) versus Jason Bergman (Nationals)

Today is my birthday. I believe it's the first time since I've been an usher that I worked on my birthday. What I know for sure is that the Cubs rarely win on my birthday, but they did today in come-from-behind fashion. When they win on your birthday, it sure makes the day even sweeter.

Final Score: Cubs 6—Nationals 4

May 6, 2007

Angel Guzman (Cubs) versus Shawn Hill (Nationals)

I noticed Ralph handing out a sheet of paper to quite a few of the ushers today. Upon investigating, I discovered that they were letters of commendation; the same one I received from Vic last year. I was a little miffed and surprised that I didn't receive one from Ralph, as he always has such praise for my work. When I saw him later, I asked him what they were, (although I already knew), and he told me that he wrote some up yesterday. I asked him what it takes to receive one, and he told me continuous good work. He followed that up by saying I will get one if I "keep on doing what I'm doing." Now, I'm even more miffed. Was the implication that I'm not as good as those he gave one to? I think not.

Later in the game Ralph brought me an ABCDE Card. As noted before, these cards are awarded to ushers who have provided outstanding service and are worth five "performance points" (whatever the hell those are) and $5 in Cubs Bucs. I'm guessing that he overlooked me when he gave out the commendations and tried to assuage his guilt by giving me the card.

Final Score: Cubs 4—Nationals 3

Daryle Ward knocked in the winning run in the bottom of the tenth.

May 18, 2007

Ted Lilly (Cubs) versus Mark Buehrle (White Sox)

The names of ushers who scored one hundred percent on the annual written exam that we are given each March at our training session were announced today —there were thirteen of them. We acknowledged those colleagues with a well-deserved round of applause. The few hundred or so of us who did NOT score one hundred percent were not told our scores. It was then that I realized that I've never been told my score. Any educator knows feedback is vital to the learning process. I wonder if they ever take any action against people who do poorly on the test.

Final Score: Cubs 6—White Sox 3

May 19, 2007

Jason Marquis (Cubs) versus Javier Vazquez (White Sox)

I'm always amazed by fans who are sitting behind the net behind home plate and who, every time the bat boy has a ball in his hand, go crazy trying to get his attention to throw them the ball. What do they expect him to do.....throw it THROUGH the net?

I worked with Luellen again today. She really is beginning to show her age (she'll be ninety-four in August). She asked me to trade her aisle for my cross-aisle today so that she wouldn't have to get up and down as much. Compare this with her ninety-three year old pal, Esther, who I worked with yesterday, who still has the energy of a thirty-nine year old. Esther still leads her section through the "YMCA" dance when it's played by the organist.

Final Score: Cubs 11—White Sox 6

Derrek Lee hit a pinch hit grand slam in the bottom of the eighth to seal the victory.

May 20, 2007

Carlos Zambrano (Cubs) versus Nick Masset (White Sox)

Today was the final game of the Cubs-Sox series. I worked all three and don't know whether I'm proud or disappointed to say that there was not a lot of tension between the two groups of fans. Yeah, there was the expected taunting of each other, but nothing serious. This series remains; however, one of the more exciting matchups of the season.

I talked to a man from Oakland, California today who was thrilled to be at Wrigley for the first time. He was laughing as he noted that he got a terrific price on his round trip ticket--$119, but wound up paying almost as much

($100) for the game ticket.

After a forty-five minute rain delay, with very few fans in the park, Ralph told those of us in the upper boxes to go down and "triple up" in all of the aisles in the club boxes. Even the old-timers said they don't remember ever doing this. Of course, there was no explanation as to what prompted these instructions.

Final Score: White Sox 10—Cubs 6

May 28, 2007

Sean Marshall (Cubs) versus Byung-Hyun Kim (Marlins)

While at dinner at a restaurant in Chicago's Edison Park neighborhood this weekend, our waitress asked me if I worked at Wrigley Field and if my name is Bruce. Upon my affirmative reply, she informed me that the hostesses recognized me from a game they were at a few weeks prior, but were embarrassed to say anything. I told her to send them over. When they arrived, we had a nice conversation and reflected on the game they were at. I guess I'm a celebrity in my own right. I offered them an autograph, but they declined.

I worked with Esther again today. She continues to amaze me; she's sharp as a tack, and her memory is better than mine. Her "regulars" love her, always greeting her with a big hug and kiss. A fan started to go into the cross-aisle to get to the men's room when Esther told him the aisle was closed. (The game had started, so we had closed the cross-aisle.) He started to argue with her, but she won the argument. She commented to me after her conversation with him that "he wouldn't have to go to the bathroom so often if he would stop drinking so much beer."

Jesse Jackson and his family were in our section today. A lot of people wanted to say hello, get an autograph, etc. He was pretty good about it. He did put up a stink when May wouldn't let him through her cross-aisle (17). But then again, so do many non-celebrities.

Jackson was showered with promotional gifts from Cubs management. That's crazy—what the hell does he need that stuff for? Why can't they save it for some kid in the upper deck or something?

Final Score: Marlins 5—Cubs 3

May 30, 2007

Ted Lilly (Cubs) versus Sergio Mitre (Marlins)

I worked by the Cubs bullpen today. I noticed that Don, a crowd control guy was stationed at the wall of my aisle.

"I didn't know we stationed someone down there," I said.

"It's something new," he said. "Ever since the bullpen pitchers have been stinking it up, they've been putting someone here to protect them."

In the seventh inning, two very cute girls walked down the aisle and sat in the first row right by Don. I followed them because I hadn't seen their tickets. Don waved me off, indicating they were OK. Funny how that works.

I talked to two foreign men today; one from Germany, the other from Holland. I asked them what language they converse in, assuming they'd say German or Dutch. They told me English. Go figure. The German guy lives here; the Dutch guy is visiting and told me how much he likes Chicago. He went on to say he just got back from a short trip to

New York City and how much better Chicago is.

Final Score: Marlins 9—Cubs 0

June 1, 2007

Carlos Zambrano (Cubs) versus Kyle Davies (Braves)

Quote of the day: a youngster asking his dad, "Where's the scoreboard?" The kid, obviously, was used to the typical electronic scoreboards at most other ballparks.

Final Score: Braves 8—Cubs 5

June 2, 2007

Rich Hill (Cubs) versus Chuck James (Braves)

Today was the day after the big fight between two Cubs, Carlos Zambrano and Michael Barrett. The fist-fight that left Barrett with six stitches in his lip and two black eyes has been the headline on all the news shows and highlighted in the newspapers and the internet since it took place. It was, of course, the topic of everyone's conversation at the park to-day—everywhere from the ushers' locker room to every seat in the stands. Everyone has an opinion. I don't remember this much hub-bub since the Bartman incident in 2003.

Meanwhile, the circus-like atmosphere continues. The Cubs have been playing like clowns for several weeks, making all kinds of physical and mental errors. Everyone has been waiting for Lou Piniella, the Cubs new manager to demonstrate his infamous short temper since the season began. Well, he finally showed us today. He argued a call by the third base umpire who called Angel Pagan out on a close play. Piniella ranted and raved, kicked dust, yelled, threw his cap, and more. He was ejected, as you would expect, and the fans were going crazy. It was McDonald's mug give away day, and hundreds of bleacher fans threw their mugs on the field. The umpires cleared the field of all players while the grounds crew cleaned up. It truly was a circus.

It was a good tip day—$14; my first tips this year. I'm not sure why, but I think I got more individual tips today than any other. I don't work too many Saturdays---could Saturday bring out the most generous fans? I'll have to monitor that. One guy (who did NOT tip me) thanked me for doing a good job and told me "there'll be a little something extra in my paycheck this week."

Final Score: Braves 5—Cubs 3

June 13, 2007

Sean Marshall (Cubs) versus Miguel Batista (Mariners)

James is in charge of usher assignments. Via the *Game Times* newsletter he offered us the opportunity to talk to him today if we had any questions or concerns about where we are being assigned. No one I talked to remembered him ever doing this before. In any event, I went to his office and mentioned that I preferred the left field assignment. He said, "No problem," and changed it on the computer. Right field and I should henceforth be history.

Final Score: Cubs 3—Mariners 2

June 15, 2007

Ted Lilly (Cubs) versus David Wells (Padres)

Today was Ernie Banks cap giveaway day. Usually I don't want the giveaways, but Ernie was my hero as a kid. (I can still recall going to games in the sixties, hoping that he would hit a home run. Then, after each game rushing out to the concourse to see if I could catch a glimpse of him as he walked on the catwalk back to the clubhouse.) Furthermore, it was a very cool blue hat with a "14" on it. Ushers never get any giveaways like they did in the years before I began working. To my good fortune, a friend of mine and his son were at the game, and his son didn't want his cap. I am now a proud owner.

I worked with Luellen and mentioned that Ernie was my childhood hero. She told me that hers was Rogers Hornsby! She really IS old. I guess our conversation put her in a nostalgic mood. She also reminisced that when Harry Caray was the Cubs announcer, he used to give her a kiss when he saw her. She said his kisses were of the very slobbery variety.

Final Score: Cubs 4—Padres 1

June 16, 2007

Carlos Zambrano (Cubs) versus Chris Young (Padres)

There was an SRO crowd today, as there is at so many of the games. But today, for some reason, I had a lot of empty seats in my section. Consequently, I was busier than usual chasing people out of seats that weren't theirs. It was appreciated by the fans who were legitimately there….although one guy said he'd appreciate it if I would let any attractive woman sit in the empty seat next to him.

I talked to the "singing vendor" today. He's the beer vendor who makes up lyrics about beer to whatever song the organist happens to be playing at the time. I asked him how he comes up with the words so quickly. He said it just comes to him. That's a rare talent.

A father and his young son from Atlanta were in my section today. They're planning on seeing every major league stadium in the country in the next few years. The guy told me he told his son he could start with whatever stadium the kid wanted. Wrigley was the kid's choice. Prior to the game, the guy asked me where the lineups are shown, as "you guys don't have a traditional scoreboard." He realized his mistake and said, "Oh, I guess you DO have a traditional scoreboard. It's every other stadium that doesn't."

One fan asked me where the trash cans were so he could throw out his hot dog wrapper. I told him there were some downstairs, but that it is perfectly acceptable to put stuff under his chair. He seemed surprised that that is the practice. Wonder what planet he's from.

Final Score: Padres 1—Cubs 0

(This is the game that featured Chris Young beaning Derrek Lee, and Lee charging the mound. Both were ejected after the bench-clearing brawl.)

June 25, 2007

Jason Marquis (Cubs) versus Jeff Francis (Rockies)

Today was the first day that I'm supposed to be in left field all the time. So far, so good. During the pre-game meeting, May (who, like me, is often assigned to Aisle 17) mentioned to me that she was assigned to right field for the first time in two years. Coincidence??

Prior to the game I stopped two kids who had just gotten autographs as they walked by me. I asked them whose autograph they got. They told me they didn't know and asked me if I could read the name. Kind of takes away from the thrill of the hunt, I think. Turns out it was Mike Quade, the third base coach.

Today's game was very exciting. It was the first time this season I was at a game where the Cubs had a comfortable lead from the very beginning. It was 8-3 Cubs in the eighth. A father in my section told me his young son was very excited, because he is a huge Cubs fan and has never seen the Cubs win. The kid was beginning to think he was a jinx. Wouldn't you know it, the bullpen imploded, and the Rockies took the lead 9-8 in the eighth. Miraculously, the Cubs rallied and won the game in the bottom of the ninth. The kid was ecstatic.

Final Score: Cubs 10—Rockies 9

June 29, 2007

Rich Hill (Cubs) versus Yovani Gallardo (Brewers)

I received another evaluation sheet today from Vic. He had glowing things to say about me. I think he makes it all up.

Today's song from the singing beer vendor, sung to the tune of "I Want to Hold Your Hand": "I want to pour your can."

Final Score: Cubs 6—Brewers 5

Aramis Ramirez hit a two-run homer in the bottom of the ninth to win it.

June 30, 2007

Sean Marshall (Cubs) versus Ben Sheets (Brewers)

T-shirt sighted: A Mark Prior jersey with a Red Cross symbol marked through the 22 (Prior's number). A humorous reference to the fact that Prior has been on the DL for years.

As I was handing a youngster a sticker that has the Cubs logo on it, a fan said, "Hey, I have that sticker", and he proceeded to lift his shirt and reveal a tattoo of the logo on his back.

The singing beer vendor mimicked the NBC signature three-note chime "Ice cold beer", as he poured a beer for a fan who was wearing an NBC shirt.

Quote of the day from a father to his son who had asked dad for some cotton candy: "Cotton candy is against our religion."

Final Score: Brewers 13—Cubs 4

July 13, 2007

Carlos Zambrano (Cubs) versus Jason Jennings (Astros)

Today was a day of requested favors from various employee groups. The team chiropractor asked if he could sit in my section. We had a nice conversation. In addition, I talked to a CTA train conductor (CTA employees get in the park for free) that I had allowed to sit in the section. Soon after, I had a Chicago fireman ask to sit there. He had his wife and three kids with him. I had to draw the line somewhere and did so with him.

Final Score: Cubs 6—Astros 0

July 15, 2007

Jason Marquis (Cubs) versus Wandy Rodriguez (Astros)

Sign of the day: "My husband sold my car so that he could buy us these tickets."

Made it to the bright lights of the Wrigley Field Scoreboard, courtesy of the Cubs' generous offer to have ushers picture taken with their name on the scoreboard

With my son Jason in the Wrigley dugout during a tour of Wrigley Field (before I was an usher)

My son Jason's first Cubs game (9/2/80) at the age of 3.

With Harry Caray at Harry's Chicago Restaurant (9/30/88)

On a tour of Wrigley Field (before I was an usher)

Cameron popping the question to Karen

With the newly engaged couple Karen and Cameron

With Cubs fans Dawn and Michelle

On my way to a pre-game Crowd Control meeting

Turn Back the Clock Day, June 2008

I talked to a guy who told me he attended the seventh game of the 1945 World Series when he was fifteen years old. Not too many left on this earth who can make that claim.

Final Score: Cubs 7—Astros 6

July 16, 2007

Rich Hill (Cubs) versus Tim Lincecum (Giants)

Barry Bonds and the Giants are in town. Bonds is currently five home runs away from breaking Hank Aaron's all-time record. Our pre-game meeting included a litany of instructions regarding how to handle the anticipated Bonds-hecklers. It's a shame one man who could be doing so much good for the game causes so much consternation. There was a media circus on the field during pre-game because of Bonds. The media were disappointed when it was announced that Bonds would not be playing today.

Jesse Jackson was in the crowd again. Man, he manages to be wherever headlines are going to be made....even if it has nothing to do with his cause.

Sign of the day was created by a woman from Shreveport, Louisiana. She knew that both infielders Ryan Theriot and Mike Fontenot both attended LSU. She had a great sign in LSU colors that referenced the two players' French heritage. It had their names followed by the words "geaux Cubs".

Final Score: Cubs 3—Giants 2
Aramis Ramirez hits a late two-run double to win it.

July 18, 2007

Carlos Zambrano (Cubs) versus Matt Cain (Giants)

The giveaway today was a reusable grocery bag from

Whole Foods. Luellen commented that she would really like one. Turns out some fans had left two at their seats. She directed me (not asked; directed) to go and get them so if the fans didn't return, she could have one. Well, the fans didn't return. She told me I could keep one, too. I told her I didn't really want it. I was going to give it to a fan after the game, but told her she could have the second one, too, thinking she wouldn't want two. To my surprise, she took them both.

Luellen is always in a hurry to get the game over with, getting frustrated if the game is slow, or if, God forbid, it goes to extra innings. She told me today that she especially likes to have Thursday games end early, as Thursdays are cocktail nights back at the retirement home.

I saw a fan today who had a dozen or so autographs on his Cubs jersey. All of his autographs were signed in magic marker and then sewn-over, so that they never fade away. Smart.

Final Score: Cubs 12—Giants 1

August 1, 2007

Rich Hill (Cubs) versus Jamie Moyer (Phillies)

The guy who sang the National Anthem today walked past me after finishing his performance. He's an older guy who hails from Idaho. I complemented him on his rendition. He told me that he's sung the Anthem at every major league park in the country—a total of sixty-two times. Said that Wrigley is his favorite. He mentioned that in addition to his ballpark gigs, he's performed at over 1,700 funerals!

Quote of the day from a vendor who was selling crackerjack and licorice ropes (probably the items that yield the fewest sales): "Get your licorice ropes and crackerjack; don't spend it all on beer, y'all."

By winning today, the Cubs claimed first place for the first time this year. When the game ended, the fans went nuts. It was quite exciting. The past couple of months, if the Cubs win, they play the song: "Go Cubs Go" which was written by Steve Goodman and very popular with Cubs fans in the eighties. Today, they played it for what must have been at least five minutes as the fans celebrated the sweet taste of first place.

Final Score: Cubs 5—Phillies 4

August 5, 2007

Jason Marquis (Cubs) versus Tom Glavine (Mets)

During today's pre-game meeting our boss announced recipients of years-of-service pins. Forty-nine of us are still here from my five-years-of-service group. The boss said that that's a lot; I'm guessing it has something to do with the fact that our first year was the 2003 almost-made-it-to-the-World Series year which addicted us. There were about fifteen 10-year people, four 15-year people and Penny who has been there twenty years. She must have started during the Andy Frain days, before the Cubs took over the security responsibilities.

Nora was the supervisor in left field today. She announced that she wanted to do something different and so she assigned people to locations in alphabetical order based on first name. How silly. I wound up being assigned to Aisle 6, but worked out a trade with Shirley who had been assigned to 17. I've been working 17 a lot lately, as several of the supervisors now assign it to me pretty automatically. It's really, in my estimation, the best assignment in the park, next to Aisle 16 which is the field access aisle for anyone with clearance to go on the field. A lot of my colleagues have asked me how I can tolerate working with Luellen, but as I've mentioned she likes me and we've become quite a team. It's a given now that I work the aisle, and she, the cross-aisle even though our official assignments are the reverse of that.

Today was the last of a three-game set with the Mets. This was an unusually difficult weekend to work. Any battle with the despised Mets is tough, but there were an awful lot of Mets fans in attendance for this series. I'm hypothesizing that this is probably because Lollapalooza, a well-known national music festival was held this weekend, and so a lot of New Yorkers decided to come to town for both weekend events.

The Mets took two of the three games, and Tom Glavine wound up winning his 300th game. It was nice to be at a game with such historical significance.

The Cubs' Alfonso Soriano, the $138 million dollar man, hurt his leg early in the game and may be out for quite a while. That really hurts. So, all in all, it was a tough weekend.

On the other hand, I got several tips this weekend. Those New Yorkers still tip. They also tend to offer bribes more than folks from other cities. As I respectfully turned down one elderly couple's offer, I overheard the woman muttering, "This sure ain't Shea Stadium."

Final Score: Mets 8—Cubs 3

August 15, 2007

Ted Lilly (Cubs) versus Phil Dumatrait (Reds)

While wiping the seats down before the game, the organist was playing "If They Could See Me Now". I had to laugh…thinking of my friends who know that I'm not very big on cleaning.

Because the game started late, beer sales were limited because of the "no beer sales after 9:20pm" rule. I saw a couple of guys order more than one, as if they were planning for hibernation.

"If I leave the park and come back," one guy asked me, "Can I re-use this ticket?"

"No," I told him. "Unless there are extenuating circumstances."

"There are," he said. "There's no more beer in here, and lots of it in the bars across the street."

Final Score: Reds 11—Cubs 9

August 17, 2007

Rich Hill (Cubs) versus Braden Looper (Cardinals)

Once again today, fans that I had let stay caught a foul ball. Had I made them move to their correct seats, they never would have gotten it.

Sometimes, so many coincidences occur, it's eerie. Today, a fan asked me what I did in my "previous life." I told him of my career in college admissions. He then told me that he was the registrar at Purdue for many years. The guy in the row behind him overheard our conversation and chimed in that his sister is the Director of Admissions at St. Xavier. Fifteen minutes later, a former colleague of mine, currently the registrar at Bradley University showed up to say hi. It must have been Admissions Officers Day at the ballpark.

And speaking of theme days at the ballpark, one of the vendors commented to me that it must be "weak kidney day" because he noticed that so many fans weren't in their seats; he surmised that they were all in the bathroom. Lousy day for him.

Great day for the Cubs, though, as they beat the Cardinals in the first of a very important four game series. With the win, the Cubs took over first place and watched the Cardinals fall three games behind them. It was a playoff-like atmosphere—very electric!

Final Score: Cubs 2—Cardinals 1

August 19, 2007

After a long rain delay, the game was finally called after only three innings had been played. The Cubs brass knew they were going to call the game a good half-hour before it was "officially" called and announced to the crowd. We knew this because several ushers saw the Cardinals leave their dugout about thirty minutes before the announcement. Some of us hypothesized that this was done in order to sell more concessions. Beer is a huge revenue producer.

Unlike previous years when there was a rain delay, I noticed that very few people asked me if I knew whether the rain was expected to stop soon so that they could determine if the game would be called. Then it dawned on me—many people had cell phones and blackberries to check the weather forecast themselves. We had 40,000 weathermen in the crowd!

August 20, 2007

Ted Lilly (Cubs) versus Joel Pineiro (Cardinals)

As if yesterday's weather wasn't bad enough (my shoes and socks had been soaked through from all the rain), we had more of the same today. But at least they got the game in.

Talked to a young father and his son who were sitting in second row club box seats. I had showed them to the same seats on Friday. The dad mentioned they were in town from Seattle. I asked how he got the same great seats for the two games. He said they were his family's season tickets—his grandfather bought the seats in 1942!

Final Score: Cardinal 6—Cubs 4

August 29, 2007

Carlos Zambrano (Cubs) versus Ben Sheets (Brewers)

I noticed last week that Jay, my locker partner of the past couple of years hasn't been around. Naturally, nobody in the office knew anything about it—even Debra who is in charge of personnel. Drew overheard me inquiring and told me Jay had a bad back. He also said that Jay doesn't think he'll be back this season. I left a message in the office to ask Jay to give me a call, since they (understandably) can't give me his phone number.

Found out today that Lenny, the eighty-something year old husband of Justeen, another usher, is in the hospital with stomach cancer and that the prognosis is not very good. Lenny and Justeen have been ushers for nineteen years. Both are such nice people.

George Will was at the game today, sitting with John Mc-

Donough in Dick and Sally's section. Mr. Will is a prominent political commentator and author who happens to be an avid Cubs fan. His political views lean heavily to the right. Both Dick and Sally are quite liberal. The three of us shared a laugh, agreeing that the only redeeming thing about Will is that he is a Cubs fan.

Final Score: Brewers 6—Cubs 1

August 31, 2007

Sean Marshall (Cubs) versus Wandy Rodriguez (Astros)

I talked to one of the FanPhoto photographers (the people who offer to take your picture and put it on the Cubs website). We were commenting on the beautiful weather, and I said all baseball games should be played during the day. She agreed. When I mentioned that it used to be that way at Wrigley, she looked at me curiously and asked what I meant. Turns out she had no idea that there was a time when Wrigley didn't have lights. I AM getting old!

And speaking of that…..sign seen today: "I've never been on cable before." Guess the young girl holding it has been on regular TV, but was hoping for more today.

Final Score: Astros 6—Cubs 1

September 1, 2007

Jason Marquis (Cubs) versus Troy Patton (Astros)

Was having a conversation today with a guy of about thirty who was remarking about what a great job I have. I agreed. The conversation took an unusual turn, though. Instead of going on to say that he looked forward to a time when he could do this job, he told me HIS dream job would be on the grounds crew—mowing the lawn. He was almost salivating as he spoke.

Today was an unusual 12:00 start. Overheard a beer vendor shouting: "Breakfast."

A helpful fan pointed out that I had some sunscreen that I hadn't rubbed in well enough on my face. Wonder how long I'd been walking around like that.

Final Score: Cubs 4—Astros 3

September 17, 2007

Rich Hill (Cubs) versus Bronson Arroyo (Reds)

John Cusak was sitting in our section today. Sally and I agreed that anyone who makes the kind of money he does should be able to afford a better hair dye job on his hair.

The Cubs won the game today 7-6 in the bottom of the ninth. The crowd went insane—it was electric. Additionally, it kept the Cubs one game ahead of the second place Brewers.

Employees of the year were named today. Ernie, a kid who started the same year I did and who has been my buddy since our first orientation, won usher of the year. He's a good kid—always a smile on his face. When I met him five years ago, he mentioned that he had dropped out of high school. Since that time, he has completed his GED, but I don't think he is pursuing college. Think I need to talk to him about that. Ralph (again) and Cindy won supervisors of the year--- both well deserved.

Final Score: Cubs 7—Reds 6

September 21, 2007

Jason Marquis (Cubs) versus Paul Maholm (Pirates)

It was unusually warm for a mid-September day--close to ninety degrees. Two guys sitting together in my section apparently dressed by the calendar and not the weather forecast; they both were wearing long sleeve sweaters. Unfazed, they didn't run to the gift shop to purchase t-shirts.

Sign of the day: "School-2 Cubs-1". I couldn't understand what that meant. I was going with the assumption that it referred to some kind of score. Alan, working nearby me, explained it meant school comes second to the Cubs first priority.

When I submitted my schedule early in the year, I knew that the Jewish holiday of Yom Kippur began tonight. I scheduled to work anyway, deciding that, if necessary, I'd just leave the game early in order to get home in time to honor the holiday. I've spent the entire month trying to determine a plan to get out early. I wound up concocting a story for Penelope, my supervisor that I aggravated a leg injury and was experiencing a lot of pain and wanted to leave. Well intended, she suggested I go get an Advil. (OK, now what?) I told her that I had taken a pain pill that morning and wasn't supposed to mix medications. (Boy, I'm quick!) Penelope told me no problem and found a replacement for me. I feel guilty— I should have told them prior to today that I was going to have to leave early. Ironically, Alan, one of the few ushers who I believe to be Jewish, was working next to me today. He didn't leave early.

Final Score: Cubs 13—Pirates 8

September 23, 2007

Carlos Zambrano (Cubs) versus Tom Gorzelanny (Pirates)

On this last home game of the season, the gates had only been open for a few minutes when a guy who I've seen a lot over the years walked down the aisle. He's one of these guys who walks around like he owns the place. I sure pegged him right. I asked him if I could see his ticket. He replied, "No, can I see yours?" I asked him again. He begrudgingly took it out of his pocket and mumbled something about being a ticket holder for thirty years.

Not much later, I was standing in front of the wall and he said, "Get out of the way." I told him that it was my job to stand there in order to prevent anyone from jumping onto the field. He said that I was blocking his view of batting practice. I again explained that I was assigned to stand by the wall. (He easily could have moved to any other seat, as it was about 11:45, and not very crowded yet.) He asked who my supervisor was, and I told him it was Penny. I flagged down a crowd control (Carmella) and explained what was going on. She proceeded to explain to him that I was simply doing my job, and that I had to stand by the wall. This made him even madder, and he asked for the name of her supervisor.

Penny arrived a short time later. I told her that I had moved up one step and things had cooled down. She wanted to talk to him, though, saying she needed some excitement in her day. He yelled at her as much, if not more than Carmella and me. He told her that he would talk to his buddy, the director of stadium operations about all this. By the time that drama ended, a lot more fans were arriving, so I was busy tending to them; my standing in his way was no longer an issue. I did spend a few more minutes down there, though, and while I was there, he made a phone call and asked the person on the other end to look in his phone directory, call Sam Zell (the brand new owner of the Tribune) and ask Sam to give him a call. Coincidence in timing? I think not.

Penny later told me that she informed Pete Robinson about what had happened. He laughed about it and mentioned that the guy works for the Tribune.

Everyone is scoreboard watching these days, with the Cubs fighting it out with the Brewers for the division title. Today, the Brewers played the Braves. When the scoreboard keeper posted a "4" for the Braves late in their game, giving them the lead, a tremendous roar went out from the crowd. The crowd then spontaneously started performing the Braves' notorious "Tomahawk Chop." It seemed everyone in the park was mocking the Chop. It was hilarious, and at the same time very emotional, as it spoke volumes about Cubs fans' passion for their team.

The Cubs won; a great game, and a great way to end their home season. (The Brewers lost, leaving the Cubs' Magic Number at 4.) Fans stuck around for a long time, hoping, I think that the team would come back on the field. That never happened. But after a while, about six Cubs came out on the field to have pictures taken with a few kids from the Chicago Boys and Girls Club (apparently, a planned event.) As the Cubs walked back to the dugout, a couple of them started tossing caps, wrist bands, etc. to the fans. One of the wrist bands deflected off one fan onto me. There was a mad rush for it. I grabbed it and handed it to a kid.

The next moment, I looked up and there was my buddy from the Tribune, red as a beet, yelling something about another fan crawling all over him, and why the hell didn't I do something about it. One of the crowd control staff who was standing on the dugout stepped in to intercede, and the guy started telling both of us how terrible we are at our jobs. He then demanded that we clear the aisle so he could leave. Out of nowhere, Penny showed up, and got rid of him. He sure helped me usher (pun intended) the regular season out with a bang.

I had to ask a fan who was standing on a seat to get down. A fan next to me yelled, "Yeah, we need the seats for the post-season." Everyone nearby laughed. She told me I could use that line any time I wanted.

Final Score: Cubs 8—Pirates 0

October 6, 2007

Rich Hill (Cubs) versus Livan Hernandez (Diamondbacks)

Well…the Cubs made it to the playoffs, having clinched the division title in Cincinnati last week. They had been the favorite in this series against the Diamondbacks. It shouldn't have surprised anyone, then, when they proceeded to lose the first two in Phoenix. They reverted to their April/May form, leaving a lot of men on base.

My supervisor for today, Nora had assigned me to Aisle 9, but Luellen shortstopped her and told her she'd really like to work with me. Nora accommodated, so I wound up working in my favorite spot for what turned out to be the final game of the season.

Yes, the Cubs lost, playing just as poorly as they did in the first two games. The Diamondbacks hit a home run on the first pitch of the game, and it was downhill from there.

Working Aisle 17 so much this season, I got to know a

couple of the season ticket holders. However, it wasn't until to-day that I learned how few of them actually come to the games. Today, for the playoffs they were all here (I know this because Luellen knows almost every one of them.) Most of these people are dripping in money.

Perhaps the funniest part of the evening (I needed SOME humor) occurred when the owners of a nearby tavern showed up. One of them is about sixty, the other about eighty-five. The latter walked with a cane. Luellen remarked that she was sur-prised they got to the game so early. She said that the older guy goes to the bathroom so often; it was silly for him to get there so early. And, she said, she should know about these things. Turns out the guy only went one time. He must have been wearing his diaper.

Final Score: Diamondbacks 5—Cubs 1

THE SIXTH INNING–
THE 2008 SEASON

TEAM RECORD: 97-64
STANDING: 1ST PLACE
MANAGER: LOU PINIELLA
ATTENDANCE: 3,300,200

Training 2008

I learned today that Lenny, Justeen's husband passed away over the break. He was such a nice guy. I'm happy to report that Justeen, like Louise did when Oliver passed away, came back for another season.

In the offseason John McDonough left the Cubs to become president of the Blackhawks, and it was announced today that Ralph had been promoted to serve as a liaison between our boss and the new executive. We'll miss Ralph in the stands, but it's a well-deserved promotion.

March 31, 2008

Carlos Zambrano (Cubs) versus Ben Sheets (Brewers)

Another Opening Day. One of the warmer ones, as it was in the fifties, but the game was delayed twice because of rain.

Cindy was my supervisor, and I'm pleased to report that she remembered my request to work Aisle 17.

Today is the day they unveiled the statue of Ernie Banks. He was honored during pre-game ceremonies. Hank Aaron, Billy Williams, Fergie Jenkins, and (surprise, surprise) Jesse Jackson were on the field with Ernie. The ceremony lacked some of the emotion that similar ones have evoked, probably because of the rain. Also, rumor has it that Ernie wasn't feeling well—he sounded very hoarse when he spoke.

Senator Durbin (who I exchanged some small talk with, because he came over to say hello to Luellen) and the Governor were in the house today.

Final Score: Brewers 4—Cubs 3

Kosuke Fukudome hit a homer in the ninth to tie it in his first game as a Cub, but the Brewers won it in the tenth.

April 3, 2008

Ryan Dempster (Cubs) versus David Bush (Brewers)

It was a beautiful day today—in the mid-sixties. Because it was a 12:05 start, it was a bit cool at the onset. As the day went on, people started stripping off their jackets, etc., making it somewhat difficult to recognize whether they were in my section as they walked to and from their seats. Suddenly, for example, the guy who entered my section in a green long sleeved jacket was now wearing a yellow t-shirt. Guess I rely more on clothing for cues than I had realized.

Final Score: Cubs 6—Brewers 3

Best Seat In The House

April 18, 2008

Rich Hill (Cubs) versus Ian Snell (Pirates)

I asked Helene why she was wearing winter gloves when it was quite warm out. She told me she wears them all the time now.

"I don't like handling the tickets when fans give them to me," she said, "because people spit all over 'em."

I get such a kick out of her.

Quote of the day from a peanut vendor: "Get your peanuts. No ID required."

T-shirt of the day with a breast cancer logo on it worn by a young woman: "Safe at second base."

Final Score: Cubs 3—Pirates 2

April 19, 2008

Jason Marquis (Cubs) versus Tom Gorzelanny (Pirates)

A woman in my section works for the Pittsburgh Pirates in the special events department. She was talking about some of the between-innings entertainment for which she is responsible. They're especially proud of the canon that shoots hot dogs into the stands. She asked what we do between innings. When I told her not much, she wasn't surprised, realizing that we fill the house every day without having to rely on those types of gimmicks.

Final Score: Cubs 13—Pirates 1

April 20, 2008

Ryan Dempster (Cubs) versus Zach Duke (Pirates)

Bonnie Hunt was at the game today, taping some stuff for her upcoming talk show. As Cindy was reading the day's

133

assignments, Bonnie came over to her and asked if she could read them off. Cindy agreed, and Bonnie had questions and comments for each usher as she called off his or her name. When she called my name, she asked me where I was from. I told her Buffalo Grove, and she said "I'm sorry to hear that." I'm not sure why she said that, but it led to a humorous exchange. I had to leave shortly after that, but I'm sure she drove Cindy nuts, as she was taking so long with each person.

I often ask fans when I check their tickets if they know where they are headed, meaning "Do you know where your seats are?" One thirty-something gentleman answered that question today with his own question: "Do you mean in life?" I advised him that I was a counselor before I retired, and so I could help him out in that respect too, if necessary.

Luellen pointed out that Cincinnati had just beaten Milwaukee. I asked her if she knew that by reading the scoreboard, thinking many people in their thirties can't see that far away, much less those in their nineties . She said yes. Said she only wears glasses for reading, and sometimes doesn't even need those. Amazing!

Final Score: Cubs 13—Pirates 6

April 30, 2008

Ryan Dempster (Cubs) versus Jeff Suppan (Brewers)
Kind of a football night—the weather, as well as the score. Wind-chill: about forty.

Final Score: Cubs 19—Brewers 5.

May 9, 2008

Ted Lilly (Cubs) versus Dan Haren (Diamondbacks)

Many fans continue to ask to if they can take a picture of me—sometimes with them, sometimes without. Perhaps the most unusual request today—fans wanted a picture of me holding on to this weird stuffed animal they brought with them to the game. I obliged.

Final Score: Cubs 3—Diamondbacks 1

May 10, 2008

Ryan Dempster (Cubs) versus Max Scherzer (Diamondbacks)

First time in all my years that I had a case of duplicate tickets. Two sets of fans had identical tickets (both were the "printed at home" variety). I had to refer the situation to crowd control who wound up escorting one of the groups to the ticket office. It looked like they were being marched off to jail. I'm not sure how they decided which group got to stay. I never did hear what happened to the jailbirds.

Final Score: Cubs 7—Diamondbacks 2

May 11, 2008

Sean Gallagher (Cubs) versus Edgar Gonzalez (Diamondbacks)

I worked in Jane's usual aisle today, as she takes Sundays off. I introduced myself to Ross, a beer vendor who's been there forever. I discovered last week that he's an oldies music aficionado, so I brought up the topic. Every time he passed me from that point on, he had some bit of music trivia to pass along. On his last visit, he told me it was nice talking to me and much nicer than Jane's only verbal exchange with him which is…"you can't go down there."

Final Score: Cubs 6—Diamondbacks 4

May 14, 2008

Ted Lilly (Cubs) versus Jake Peavy (Padres)

Esther took a day off today. Delores who always works with her put up a sign on the cross-aisle that said "Esther is fine…she just took a day off." She does this so she doesn't have to explain the situation to fans time after time. I thought that was a riot. Esther, like Luellen, is ninety-four years old. Every time she (or Luellen, for that matter) isn't at a game, her loyal fans get nervous.

Met one of my favorite celebrities today—former Cubs clubhouse manager Yosh Kowano. He was commenting on the tickets he had for the game. You'd think they'd still let him watch from the dugout.

Final Score: Cubs 8—Padres 5

May 17, 2008

Carlos Zambrano (Cubs) versus Zach Duke (Pirates)

Quote of the day came from Luellen. "What's this '*Sex in the City*' stuff?" She was referring to all the publicity about the movie that's due out soon.

Final Score: Pirates 7—Cubs 6

May 26, 2008

Ryan Dempster (Cubs) versus Chad Billingsley (Dodgers)

Tommy Lasorda was in my section today—Seat 1, Row 1 behind the Dodgers' dugout. I was explicitly told by Cindy that I was not to allow any autograph seekers near him unless Cindy found out that he would agree to sign. He told her he would, so I wound up sending two fans at a time down to meet him in between innings. Cindy told me that Lasorda could be a real asshole sometimes; that he's been known to yell at ushers, that he's moody, etc. I asked several fans that had gotten autographs what he was like, and they all said he was pleasant. Must have been one of his good days.

A moment of silence was held today, Memorial Day. I've experienced a number of these since starting, but today was perhaps the most moving, as it was a bit breezy and all you could hear were the flags flapping.

Final Score: Cubs 3—Dodgers 1

May 28, 2008

Carlos Zambrano (Cubs) versus Derek Lowe (Dodgers)

Talked to Ron, the groundskeeper who operates the balls and strikes on the scoreboard. (He's been doing this, by the way, for nineteen years.) I've referred to Ron before, noting the amazing speed with which he gets the count up on the scoreboard. I had been told that he does this by learning the various motions of each of the leagues' umpires. I asked him today if this was, indeed, how he worked his magic. He confirmed. He kidded that one day I should bet someone that his response time would slow down. Ron would then deliberately slow down (at a pre-arranged time), enabling me to win the bet. Not a bad idea.

Quote of the day comes from Ross, the beer vendor. As the PA announcer informed us that the Cubs music guys were going to play some polka music for our listening pleasure, Ross exclaimed, "Listening PLEASURE---are you kidding?"

Final Score: Cubs 2—Dodgers 1

May 30, 2008

Ted Lilly (Cubs) versus Aaron Cook (Rockies)

The day started with threatening skies and tornado warnings. The tarp was held down with sandbags in preparation for the worst. I have never seen that before. We were told to move all the box seat fans up to the grandstand when the signal was given. I've never been given instructions along those lines, either. Well—the wind gusts never came; the game started only twenty minutes late, and not a drop of rain was felt from that point on. And the place went nuts after an incredible win.

It turned out to be one of the craziest games I've worked. The Cubs came from behind 9-1 to beat the Dodgers 10-9. The game was highlighted by a six-run seventh inning by the Cubs; two of those runs came on a home run by Mark DeRosa, the fourth of five Cub homers that day. The wind was blowing out, and I knew the Cubs wouldn't be out of it until the last out. But, they held on to win.

Final Score: Cubs 10—Rockies 9

May 31, 2008

Ryan Dempster (Cubs) versus Glendon Rusch (Rockies)

I worked by the Cubs bullpen today. Before the game started, Ryan Theriot was signing autographs. He gave an autographed ball to a kid who was about ten years old. A bit later, the kid found out that three of the guys who were standing near him were US Marines. He offered one of the Marines the autographed ball,

"You deserve it," the kid said. "You're a hero."

How touching was that? The marine and his buddies signed the ball and gave it back to the kid. The kid insisted, though, that the marine keep the ball. This was one of the most poignant moments in my Wrigley tenure.

In what can only be described as pure karma, the Cubs bullpen catcher later gave the kid a bat that had been used and cracked during the game. Well deserved!

Final Score: Cubs 5—Rockies 4

June 12, 2008

Carlos Zambrano (Cubs) versus Tim Hudson (Braves)
Today was Turn-Back-the-Clock Day. It was 1948 all over again, as the Cubs and WGN celebrated sixty years of Cubs games on Channel 9. Both the Cubs and Braves wore their 1948 uniforms. Food was sold at significantly reduced prices for an hour before the game. Vendors wore 1940s clothing, as did staff from the Cubs marketing department. And we ushers….we were given straw hats to wear. As Wayne Mesmer walked past Luellen and me to announce the game from the field (as Pat Piper used to do during those years), he pointed out that straw hats were not from the 1940s.

Sign of the day: "Vote for Truman."

The PA system broke down toward the end of the game. As a result, the "Go Cubs Go" song which is now played at the end of each Cubs win could not be heard. Needless to say, lots of fans were quite disappointed. At one point though, a large contingent of fans broke out in the song a cappella. Sent a chill through the spine!

Final Score: Cubs 3—Braves 2

The winning run was scored when Reed Johnson was hit by a pitch with the bases loaded in the bottom of the eleventh.

June 20, 2008

Our boss told us that we can come to the park on July 3rd (an off-day for the team) to have our picture taken on the field, standing at home plate. The scoreboard in the background would have our name on it. Very nice gesture. What prompted this, I wonder?

My friend, Cubs Associate Walter Johnson, also wrote a song about our jobs. These are the lyrics…

Let's put the friendly in the friendly confines
Let's put a smile on all the fans
Let's make their outing a lasting memory
Let's keep 'em happy in the stands

Our pride is showing when we work together
We pledge to go that extra mile
From upper deck to scanning tickets
We want to make their day worthwhile

We don't complain in front of the folks
We come in all shapes and sizes
Braving cold, rain, and the boss' jokes
Always awaiting those fabulous prizes

Our daily effort and positive attitude,

Best Seat In The House

Pays dividends to the crowd
It pays off in gratitude
And really makes us proud

Some of us are retired, students, and teachers
And look frightened when assigned to the bleachers
When we are tired and think we can't go
We're inspired by our own Ron Santo

We welcome all when scanning tickets
Appreciate the personal touch of Mr. Ricketts
We keep our eye on underage drinking,
Supplied by friends, "what were they thinking?"

So let's put the friendly in the friendly confines
Let's put a smile on all the fans,
Let's make their outing a lasting memory
Let's keep 'em happy in the stands

(Written by Walter C. Johnson
Chicago Cubs Associate)

June 22, 2008

Ryan Dempster (Cubs) versus Javier Vazquez (White Sox)
Today was the third game of the series against the White
Sox. The Cubs won, sweeping the series. It was an incredible
three days. Each day it rained prior to the start of the game
and then the skies cleared, enabling the games to go on with
no more than a half-hour delay. Today, perhaps tellingly, a

brilliant double rainbow appeared over the right field wall.

Because this Sunday's game was pushed back to a night game in order to get the national TV dollars, a lot of people changed their drinking pattern. They had all day to hang out at the Wrigleyville bars to get drunk and then come into the park to have even more to drink (although beer vendors unanimously proclaimed that it was a very slow day---perhaps people realized Monday morning work would be here very soon). We did see quite a few fans who had obviously over-imbibed. I had to be adamant with one fan who kept getting up from his seat (he accidentally hit me in the head as I was talking to him.) Later it was very amusing watching him attempt to take pictures in his drunken stupor. He couldn't quite keep the camera steady and kept trying to focus with one eye.

Final Score: Cubs 7—White Sox 1

June 25, 2008

Ted Lilly (Cubs) versus Matt Albers (Orioles)

Caroline told me today that she loves Wrigley so much she wishes she could sleep there at night.

Quote of the day: As I showed a couple to their box seats, the husband observed, "Honey, we've arrived in heaven."

Final Score: Cubs 7—Orioles 4

June 26, 2008

Jason Marquis (Cubs) versus Redhames Liz

Today was Yosh Kowono day. After he was honored on the field during pre-game ceremonies, he walked back into the stands and wound up singing the National Anthem right next to me. I shook his hand and congratulated him after the song.

Final Score: Orioles 11—Cubs 4

July 9, 2008

Carlos Zambrano (Cubs) versus Johnny Cueto (Reds)

Esther had told a couple of us yesterday that one of our colleagues, Ginger, had passed away, and Esther had gone to the funeral. Imagine my surprise when I saw Ginger at the pre-game meeting today. Turns out Esther had been talking about a fan named Ginger. Fortunately, another one did NOT bite the dust.

Tyler is one of our more colorful ushers. He started the same year I did, and for the past six years he has been taking the train from his hometown in southern Illinois, not far from St. Louis. I think he stays with one of his kids in the Chicago area while the Cubs are in town. He told me today that he was in a gas station in his hometown last week, paying a bill. A woman saw his Cubs shirt and told him that she was a Cardinals fan, and hated the Cubs so much, she was going to walk outside until he was finished.

"I can't even be in the same room as a Cubs fan," she said. "I hate everything about the Cubs-- the team, the fans, Wrigley; even the ivy on the outfield wall."

She also told him of a plot to kill the ivy. Apparently, (or maybe it's just in her mind), a group of fans who sit in the bleachers take their empty beer cups to the bathroom, urinate in them, and then bring the cups back and pour the urine on the ivy. Are you kidding me?

Sign of the day: Today is NOT my birthday; NOT my first Cubs game, and my wife DIDN'T buy me these tickets.

Final Score: Cubs 5—Reds 1

July 11, 2008

Jason Marquis (Cubs) versus Matt Cain (Giants)

Luellen found a quarter on the ground today and promptly showed it to me. I remarked that I usually only find pennies. She responded, "I don't bend down for pennies."

Luellen was also offered a bribe today. I've been offered many a bribe over the years, but I was a bit surprised that someone would offer one to a ninety-four year old woman. Then she elaborated on the details of the bribe---the guy offered to donate $50 to her church if she'd let him move down.

Final Score: Cubs 3—Giants 1

July 12, 2008

Rich Harden (Cubs) versus Kevin Correia (Pirates)

I pinch hit today for Esther who took a day off. Delores, once again put up her sign that says, "Esther is fine—she's just taking the day off". This time the boss saw it and instructed her to take it down.

I'm glad I don't have to work this section too often. Esther and Delores have a system. Every time an opposing player is out, they high-five each other. Delores wanted me to keep up the tradition. I obliged.

Final Score: Cubs 8—Giants 7

Reed Johnson knocked in the winning run in the bottom of

the eleventh.

July 13, 2008

Ryan Dempster (Cubs) versus Tim Lincecum (Giants)

A well-known race car driver was sitting in my section today…Bobby somebody or other. I saw the guy signing an autograph, not knowing who the heck he was. I had to ask the guy sitting with him what his name was.

Final Score: Giants 4—Cubs 2

July 25, 2008

Ryan Dempster (Cubs) versus Josh Johnson (Marlins)

I confiscated my first beach ball today. It had been bouncing around for a minute, and I was able to get it quickly—much to the chagrin of the crowd. I suffered a few boos.

Final Score: Marlins 3—Cubs 2

July 26, 2008

Rich Harden (Cubs) versus Rich Volstad (Marlins)

A fan asked me today for my autograph. Not sure why. Maybe this is the start of something. Heard this memorable exchange too…

Beer vendor to customer: "Sorry, I only have Lite."

Customer: "What's the point?"

Final Score: Marlins 3—Cubs 2

August 1, 2008

Jason Marquis (Cubs) versus Jeff Karstens (Pirates)

Poignant moment of the day: A veteran who served in Iraq and lost both legs was introduced to the crowd prior to the singing of The National Anthem. He was then wheeled around the field in his wheelchair. Lots of tears in the audience.

Overheard from one of the young hot dog vendors: "Hot dogs. You NEED to eat." The vendor's name was Jeremy Levin (or some Jewish name like that). I could hear his mother telling him the same thing twenty years ago.

Final Score: Pirates 3—Cubs 0

August 2, 2008

Ted Lilly (Cubs) versus Paul Maholm (Pirates)

T-shirt of the day: The number 101 with a line crossed through it (referring to the fact that Cubs fans can't wait one more year to win the World Series).

One woman on the crowd control staff told me that a guy in the crowd rubbed up against her and he had a hard on. She didn't seem too perturbed about it. Glad to know she feels so comfortable sharing.

Talked to a group of guys from Iowa who were at the park today for their twenty-second annual "Cubs and Pubs" outing. Cool name for their weekend.

Final Score: Cubs 5—Pirates 1

August 5, 2008

Rich Harden (Cubs) versus Wandy Rodriguez (Astros)

I was fortunate to not have to work last night's game. It stormed like crazy—lightning, thunder, gusts of wind. There was a two hour and forty-five minute rain delay. The game resumed, but then even stormier conditions arrived. Tornado sirens went off and crowd control had to clear the park, sending everyone down to the concourse. Everyone I talked to today had horror stories to share.

Final Score: Cubs 11—Astros 7

August 6, 2008

Jason Marquis (Cubs) versus Brandon Backe (Astros)

I served as water boy before the game today. (On hot days, water is distributed to ushers before and during the game.) I happened to be going down for some water for Lu-ellen and bumped into Cindy who told me the water station hadn't been set up yet. She asked if I could help get the ball rolling. So, she, Jill and I went into the bowels of the stadium to load huge water and ice containers. I then distributed water to all of the ushers on the right field side. Not something I'd want to do every day, but it was cool to make the rounds and say hi to everyone.

Final Score: Cubs 11—Astros 4

August 8, 2008

Ted Lilly (Cubs) versus Braden Looper (Cardinals)

Today was the twentieth anniversary of the first night game at Wrigley. Commemorative caps were given out to recall the event. Even though they were cheap imitations of the original one handed out twenty years ago, it was a nice reminder.

I've always been curious about the fact that hot dog vendors now offer ketchup as well as mustard. This is perplexing because, as every Chicagoan knows, it is practically against the law to put ketchup on a hot dog in Chicago. I asked one of the vendors today about the percentage of people who ask for ketchup. He couldn't give me an exact number, but he did say that it is definitely a generational thing---that it's mostly younger people who request ketchup. And of course, out-of-towners—what do they know?

Two guys from Boston sat in my section today. (There were a lot of Red Sox fans in the crowd today, as the Red Sox were scheduled to play the White Sox at Cellular Field tonight). They were enthralled with Wrigley. One remarked, "I hope they play fifteen innings."

He almost got his wish—they played eleven.

During pre-game ceremonies today, four Navy parachutists landed at second base. Their landing was breathtaking and amazingly accurate. After the game, two of them came down by the dugout where I was working. We had a nice conversation during which I asked them what was more exhilarating—a landing or watching the Cubs win in the eleventh. Without hesitation, one said, "The Cubs, of course." The other said, "No comment."

Final Score: Cubs 3—Cardinals 2

August 9, 2008

Carlos Zambrano (Cubs) versus Todd Wellemeyer (Cardinals)

As sharp as Luellen is for a ninety-four year old, she does, indeed, have trouble remembering people, and consequently asks people for their tickets every time they leave their seat and/or return. Needless to say, that's quite annoying to some people.

Today I saw the two girls, Cubs groupies, who I got to know during my first season. They said they haven't been coming to many games in the last two years, but hoped that they would find me today. When I first got to know them they were students at Buffalo Grove High School. Now they are college seniors. Time flies.

With the Cubs doing so well, tickets are really tough to get and are going at premium prices. One guy told me today he spent $1,700 for four lower box seats.

I realized today that many former ushers come to a lot of games as fans. Whether they were fired or quit on their own accord, they still have passion for this team.

Intrigued by the ketchup conversation I had yesterday, I decided to do some investigating about fans' refreshment preferences. I asked a beer vendor for the percentage of beer sold–regular vs. light. He said it's easily seventy-five percent lite. Good thing—with all the beer that's consumed at the games, the average fan would weigh 300 pounds if all those beers were regular.

Sign of the day: "I cannot lie—this is my SECOND Cubs game. I forgot to bring my sign to the first one."

Final Score: Cardinals 12—Cubs 3

August 10, 2008

Ryan Dempster (Cubs) versus Chris Carpenter (Cardinals)

Got a $5 tip today—not all that unusual, but I think it's the first time someone has tipped me on his way out after the game. The guy must have thought I was pretty good. Nice.

T-shirt of the day seen on a Cardinals fan: "Chicago Cubs—providing an alternative to winning since 1908." Ouch, that hurts. Clever, though.

Final Score: Cubs 6—Cardinals 2

August 22, 2008
Jason Marquis (Cubs) versus John Lannan (Nationals)

Over the past few years, whenever I take a picture of fans, I've continued to tell them to say "Cubs win" when I'm about to take the shot. It's kind of become my trademark. People seem to get a kick out of it. Well, apparently my trademark has made it to Washington. Luellen's son works at one of the important institutions in Washington D.C. She told him about my "Cubs win," story and he thought it was very cool and now uses it whenever he takes pictures. For all I know, he's already used it on all kinds of dignitaries. Maybe I should patent it.

I made a record $17 in tips today…it was raining, and a lot of people were generous after I dried off their seats. Luellen was in a particularly good mood…she gave me her only tip (one dollar). As she left, she said "don't spend it all in one place."

Final Score: Nationals 13—Cubs 5

August 23, 2008
Ryan Dempster (Cubs) versus Odalis Perez (Nationals)

Luellen and I were talking to a guy who lives in Kansas City, but comes to a lot of Cubs games because he has family in Chicago. He told us that he always buys an extra ticket and gives it to a kid on the street who can't afford the cost of a game. Today he went into McDonald's and gave it to a manager to give to one of the employees. What a mensch!

Speaking of that …I've always thought how unfair it is that the kids who get baseballs tossed to them by players are the ones in the first couple of rows…the ones who probably could afford to buy the team.

It was very warm and humid today. There was a sudden rainstorm that brought huge raindrops that were freezing when they hit me. Very uncomfortable, but the rain left as quickly as it came in.

Final Score: Cubs 9—Nationals 2

August 24, 2008

Rich Harden (Cubs) versus Jason Bergman (Nationals)

Jill told me about this guy who was standing by my aisle when I got there. Apparently he's there a lot, and she wanted to warn me about him. She told me he's a "collector." That is, he yells down to visiting players and asks them for balls, bats, etc. In talking to him, I found out he has a collection of over 400 bats, 200 caps, who knows how many balls, and God knows what else. I asked him if he sells the stuff, and he told me that he doesn't. He just likes to collect the stuff. Doesn't even display it….everything is in boxes at home. The guy works for Chicago Streets and Sanitation. Need I say more?

Final Score: Cubs 6—Nationals 1

August 29, 2008

Rich Harden (Cubs) versus Joe Blanton (Phillies)

Mike Schmidt, the Hall of Fame Phillies third baseman sat in my section today. He was quite introverted, not wanting to be bothered by anyone. He looked old and seemed about half the size he was when he was playing.

A first pitch was thrown out today by a five-year-old. His name? Wrigley Fields!!

A fan in my section was quite upset because two people sitting behind him wouldn't stop talking.

"Their conversation has nothing to do with baseball," he complained.

I advised him that there wasn't much I could do about that. An inning later he and one of the "talkers" got into an altercation. As I was going down to attend to the situation, he walked past me.

"I've had it," he said. "I'm out of here"

And he left the ballpark. Doesn't take much to really piss off some people.

Final Score: Cubs 3—Phillies 2

August 31, 2008

Sean Marshall (Cubs) versus Jamie Moyer (Phillies)

A fan asked me where the nearest garbage can was. I told her that there were receptacles down in the concourse, but it's acceptable to simply place garbage under your seat—that's what everyone does. "Oh, I couldn't do that" she said. She went on to explain that she works in a movie theater where she cleans up the floors every day and was feeling empathy for whoever has to clean Wrigley. I told her Wrigley has a much more high-tech clean up system, using high power machines to do the job. Apparently, I wasn't very convincing. I saw her walk down to the concourse with garbage at least four times.

There are often groups of four young guys who show up at the park, each with one letter of the word "CUBS" painted on their chests. Today my section featured a group of three, spelling "CUB". Throughout the game they were trying to recruit people to paint an "S" on their chest. Finally, around the sixth inning, they found a willing subject. The crowd around the guys roared with approval as they painted the "S" on the guy's chest.

Presidential candidate Barak Obama recently stirred up a bit of controversy when he proclaimed that he was a White Sox fan and that Cubs fans merely come to the park to drink and have a good time; not to follow the game. Today's t-shirt of the day featured a NO OBAMA logo and the words "Cubs fans know the score."

Final Score: Phillies 5—Cubs 3

September 3, 2008
Ryan Dempster (Cubs) versus Randy Wolf (Astros)

I got to know a couple of the vendors fairly well this season. There's Ross, the guy I mentioned who looks like a hippie and knows everything about pop music. There's Walter who greets me with a big smile and a hand shake every day. Drew told me that Walter invited him to go out on his boat earlier this year. Drew has known him a bit longer—maybe I'll get an invitation next year. And there's Levi, a young orthodox Jew who attended Jewish schools through high school and is working on his engineering degree. Today Levi told that me it was his last day. He's decided to enlist in the Israeli army and leaves Sunday. He's a great young man, and I wish him the best.

Final Score: Astros 4—Cubs 0

September 17, 2008
Jason Marquis (Cubs) versus Ben Sheets (Brewers)

A young woman was oohing and aahing over Ryan Braun of the Brewers before the game. When I asked her why him, she responded, "Because I heard you're not available."

The very slight and demure Asian woman who's been meekly vending peanuts since I've been there threw a bag of peanuts to a customer today, (as peanut vendors often do). Her toss, however hit the fan in the head. Yikes! What did the fan do? Threw it back at her, of course.

Final Score: Brewers 6—Cubs 2

September 20, 2008

Ted Lilly (Cubs) versus Joel Pineiro (Cardinals)

Cubs Win!!! I've been very good about not revealing anticipation/expectations for the Cubs this year. Today, they clinched the Central Division. They've been the best team in the league since early in the year, but being a typical Cubs fan, I didn't want to jinx anything by putting any thoughts down on paper. But here are the facts. All year they've had a very strong pitching staff. All year they had timely hitting; leaving relatively few men on base....something they haven't been able to do for the past few decades. But these are the tell-tale signs of any good ball club. What's made this team special are the other signs. The balls they hit that "had eyes" and dropped for hits. The balls hit by other teams that seemed to be attracted to Cubs' gloves like magnets. And then there was the day in June when that double rainbow appeared just before game time. Maybe the hundred year anniversary of the last year they won the World Series will be THE YEAR.

After the game, there was all the fun of a division clinching celebration. I didn't get a real close-up view of the festivities, but it was a lot of fun celebrating with the fans who were allowed to stay about an hour and a half after the game ended. I did get sprayed with champagne as some of the Cubs walked by the wall trying to get some of the fans wet.

Final Score: Cubs 5—Cardinals 4

September 21, 2008

Ryan Dempster (Cubs) versus Braden Looper (Cardinals)
Quote of the day from a thirty-something guy sitting in the second row as I sat a family with three young kids in the first row: "Well, looks like we won't get any balls tossed to us today."

Final Score: Cubs 5—Cardinals 1

Early October, 2008

Well, I guess I shouldn't have put my thoughts down on paper after all. After such a great year, the Cubs imploded and lost all three games of the first round of the playoffs against the Dodgers. This team that won ninety-seven games during the regular season; this team that had the best record by far in the National League; this team that most experts picked to go all the way played like the game was foreign to them. Dempster walked seven in the first game—I don't think he walked seven all year. They made four errors in the second game. And they didn't hit at all…scoring six runs in all three games. They are now 0 and 6 in playoff games the last two years. I'm once again going through the October mourning process. It never gets any easier.

I worked both of the playoff games that were at Wrigley. At that second game, I had an interesting conversation with an AP photographer. We were lamenting about the fact that it looked like the Cubs were going to blow it another year. I asked him for his thoughts about how such a good team could blow it like this. He had a very insightful response. He said that he thinks the Cubs have more pressure on them than any other team in baseball; that the whole world wants the Cubs to win. No other team has that kind of pressure. That line of thinking makes a lot of sense and helps to ease the pain a bit. Just a bit.

Sitting in my section at that second game was Mark Cuban—one of the finalists to buy the Cubs. I was so very impressed with him. He's a guy who has all the money in the world but couldn't be more down to earth. He signed autographs and posed for pictures for everyone who asked. He was the cheerleader of the section—urging fans around him to get up and cheer the team on despite their horrific performance. Around the fifth (the Cubs were already pretty much out of the game) I jokingly asked him if he still is interested in purchasing the team.

"Of course," he replied, "there's nothing better than this."

Later in the game, a couple of guys were standing in the aisle talking to him. I asked them to please clear the aisle, and they started politely arguing with me, saying they really wanted to finish their conversation with him.

"Hey," Cuban said to me, "if you want to keep your job when I take over, you should let them be."

"OK, I replied. "Why don't you guys go down to the first

row and have a seat."

Cuban thought that was funny.

THE SEVENTH INNING—
THE 2009 SEASON

TEAM RECORD: 83-78
STANDING: 2ND PLACE
MANAGER: LOU PINIELLA
ATTENDANCE: 3,168,859

April 13, 2009

Ted Lilly (Cubs) versus Ubaldo Jimenez (Rockies)

Another Opening Day that brought frigid temperatures. I just looked back at my previous Opening Day entries to see if there had been one as bad as today's. Turns out it's a contest. Today's forty degree or so temps were accompanied by strong winds and a rain that started about two hours before game time and continued all day. The game was delayed and didn't begin until 2:30 or so. By the time we got out of there, it was almost 6:00. So I spent seven hours battling the elements and hoping my toes wouldn't fall off.

The good news is no ushers died during the off-season (at least none that I'm aware of). The bad news is that Vern, one of the nicest ushers, was diagnosed with cancer. I saw him at training last week and immediately surmised that

he must be quite ill, as he lost so much weight. Turns out
he has cancer of the esophagus and is about a third of the
way through his treatment. He seems optimistic, but said at
training that he won't be able to work for several weeks.

Overheard quote of the day. in the very long line to get
in the men's room: "They must have put extra diuretics in
the beer today."

Final Score: Cubs 4—Rockies 0

April 15, 2009

Rich Harden (Cubs) versus Jason Marquis (Rockies)

I was assigned Vern's aisle today. I've never worked that
section before, as Vern works most games. Great assignment,
but so sad that I had to get it.

Quote of the day from a fan as he handed me his ticket:
"I thought only eighty-year old ladies have these jobs."

Final Score: Rockies 5—Cubs 2

April 17, 2009

Carlos Zambrano (Cubs) versus P.J. Walters (Cardinals)

Rose gave me some personnel updates she'd heard about.
Rob, who is about ninety, worked his nineteenth Opening
Day earlier this week. He quit immediately afterward, finally
caving in to the weather. He also works the Bulls games at
the United Center and since it's always warm in there, decided to just work basketball games.

I spent a lot of time talking to a Cardinals employee. He's
an "analyst," a guy who makes predictions about players' success based exclusively on statistics. He said that only about
four or five major league teams employ people to do what he

does. He was very nervous today, because one of his predicted successes was making his major league pitching debut. The twenty-four year old pitcher gave up three runs in the first couple of innings, but then the Cubs had difficulty hitting his change-up which the analyst had been elaborating on. The pitcher left the game with a one run lead in the fifth or so. The "analyst" seemed happy.

I spent some time talking to a new crowd control guy named Lonnie who was beaming the whole day. He's been a Cubs fan for all of his twenty or so years and was like a kid in a candy store as he strolled the aisles.

I was "evaluated" today by Vic. This is part of the new evaluation system whereby ushers are rated randomly and periodically. I got a perfect score. Ain't I the shit?

Final Score: Cubs 8—Cardinals 7

Alfonso Soriano hit a two-run homer in the bottom of the eighth to win it.

May 1, 2009

Rich Harden (Cubs) versus Graham Taylor (Marlins)

I was assigned to the last aisle located in the right field corner today. It's been a long time since I was so far out. Reason: a new supervisor, Frank didn't know me. I talked to him and told him I usually am much closer in. He made a note for next time.

Final Score: Cubs 8—Marlins 6

May 2, 2009

Ted Lilly (Cubs) versus Anibel Sanchez (Marlins)

Quote of the day from a fan here from Nashville. After seeing the Cubs win the first of three games he bought tickets for, he remarked, "Where's the nearest church?—I want to pray they play as well the next two days."

Final Score: Cubs 6—Marlins 1

May 3, 2009

Carlos Zambrano (Cubs) versus Ricky Nolasco (Marlins)

Uniform number 31 representing Fergie Jenkins and Greg Maddux was retired today. Jenkins' number 31 was put on the left field flagpole, and Maddux's was on the right field pole.

T-shirt of the day: An image of a man's skeletal system. A Cubs logo appears where the heart would normally be.

Sight of the day: Newly acquired Milton Bradley signing autographs by the Cubs dugout just before game time. Very nice, especially from a guy who supposedly is a real jerk. (Ironically, I had told a couple of kids that they couldn't go down there; that players never give autographs just before game time.)

Final Score: Cubs 6—Marlins 4

May 14, 2009

Ryan Dempster (Cubs) versus Chad Gaudin (Padres)

Another nice sighting: Terry Sullivan, somewhat of a local celebrity (he is an attorney who often appears on WGN TV) gave his lower box seat tickets to a young kid as he left the game in the seventh inning.

Final Score: Cubs 11—Padres 3

May 24, 2009

Ted Lilly (Cubs) versus Chris Young (Padres)

Mr. T, today's guest conductor for the seventh inning stretch, shook my hand as he walked to the field. He approached me with a big grin, unlike most celebrities who do anything they can to avoid interacting with the crowd.

Ronnie Woo Woo, the infamous guy who has been walking the park yelling, "Woo, woo" for the past several years was seated in the grandstand behind me today. To say that his woo-wooing is disturbing is putting it mildly. I wanted to slug the guy from the fifth inning on.

Final Score: Padres 7—Cubs 2

May 29, 2009

Ted Lilly (Cubs) versus Chad Billingsley (Dodgers)

Was finally assigned to Aisle 17 (first time this year). Nice to be back in my favorite spot. I said hello to several season ticket owners who I hadn't seen since last year, as well as a few of the vendors who always work this area.

I also saw Andrea Silverman today. Andrea was diagnosed with cancer over the winter. Right now, she is cancer-free, but is still a bit affected by the treatments. Her spirits are good, though.

To the best of my ability, I deliberately time my breaks so that I'm gone when the opposing team is up at bat, so as to not miss any Cubs offensive heroics. Sometimes, though, the break usher comes when the Cubs are up, and I really need a potty break, so I go. Today was the second day in a row that I was on break while the Cubs were at bat. More significantly, today was the second day in a row that while I was in the bathroom, a Cubs player homered. I discovered that the noise in the bathroom is deafening when that happens. The drunk fans in the john sure know how to whoop it up.

Final Score: Cubs 2—Dodgers 1

The Cubs player who homered was Koyie Hill (in the seventh.)

May 30, 2009

Ryan Dempster (Cubs) versus Eric Stults (Dodgers)

I worked with eighty-five year old Jed for the second consecutive day today. Jed has been an usher for twenty years and worked Aisle 11 for the past several years. He told me they moved him to Cross-Aisle 17 this year because he can't read the tickets. (Ushers who work cross-aisles don't have to check tickets.)

Jed is unintentionally funny—He'll shout out Go, Cubbies" when they're not at bat, for example.

Dozens of birds filled the field toward the end of the game today. They amused the crowd and probably pissed off the players. They hung around for quite a while.

I met a guy from Palatine in Naples, Florida this past winter, and he found me at the ballpark today. I had struck up a conversation with him in Florida because he was wearing a Cubs shirt at the time. I didn't recognize him at first, but we had a great conversation.

Vern, who's been out all season undergoing treatment for cancer, showed up as a fan today. It was so good to see him. He's looking weak, but his spirits seemed good, and he is looking forward to returning to work later this summer.

Final Score: Cubs 7—Dodgers 0

June 12, 2009

Randy Wells (Cubs) versus Kevin Slowey (Twins)

There was a front page article in yesterday's *Tribune* about Tyler. The article focused on the fact that Tyler, who is seventy-nine, lives in southern Illinois and takes the train over 300 miles to Chicago for every Cubs home stand. It was a great, feel-good article that is great for Cubs PR—EXACTLY WHAT I THOUGHT WOULD BE THE CASE WHEN THE *TRIB* WANTED TO DO A STORY ON ME DURING MY FIRST YEAR AND THE CUBS THREATENED TO FIRE ME IF I DIDN'T HAVE THE STORY PULLED. Our boss even mentioned the article with a big smile at today's meeting.

Final Score: Twins 7—Cubs 4

June 17, 2009

Ryan Dempster (Cubs) versus John Danks (White Sox)

Worked the Cubs-Sox game today and was assigned to the Sox family section. That's a challenge; it's bad enough having all those Sox fans in the park, but so many devout fans who despise the Cubs in one confined space….that's a different story.

Final Score: White Sox 4—Cubs 1

June 19, 2009

Rich Harden (Cubs) versus Cliff Lee (Indians)

I've always wondered what happened to Larry, a terrific guy I got to know a bit during my first few years. I'd periodically ask other ushers if they knew what happened to him, but nobody did. Finally, today, I asked LaMont (I thought maybe he knew because they're both black—how's that for a stereotype?) LaMont said, "You mean the black guy?" I told him "yes", and he told me he passed away a few years ago. Once again, it sure would be nice if management would announce these things.

As I was eating some honeydew melon today, a fan walked past me and said, "You must have high cholesterol." I asked him what gave it away, but he refused to answer. Curious.

I worked with Dwight today who I've never worked with before even though he's been here five or six years. During one of our conversations about our experiences at the park, he said, "I could write a book." If only he knew.

Final Score: Cubs 8—Indians 7

The Cubs came back from down seven runs to win it in the bottom of the tenth.

June 20, 2009

Ted Lilly (Cubs) versus Tomo Ohka (Indians)

I've become buddies with one of the younger vendors who stops by to shoot the shit every day. I always assumed that vendors were given their assignments (both what and where they vend) based on seniority, and I was right about that. What I didn't know is that there is also a lottery system to determine who gets to sell what.

The Cubs played the Indians today, and Sara Wood, wife of Kerry Wood, who was traded to the Indians over the winter, had seats in my section. I should say she had ROWS in my section. Somehow, she and her party occupied most of two rows. The whole day was like one big party. She had friends come over to say hi throughout the game. Some stayed and sat, others just stopped by. She paid no attention to the game until Kerry came in to pitch, at which time she said to her son, "Look, Daddy's pitching." Last time I heard that phrase was when my ex said that to my son at a family picnic. Not quite the same thing, is it? Unfortunately for Sara Wood, Kerry blew the game for the Indians.

Final Score: Cubs 6—Indians 5

July 3, 2009

Carlos Zambrano (Cubs) versus Jeff Suppan (Brewers)

Many of the ushers (me included) spend a lot of time attempting to determine how the supervisors make their assignments. We assume assignments are made based on seniority and the supervisors' assessment of the employee's work. But Nora likes to be creative with her assignments. Today, she came up with a new one: she made assignments based on ushers' height.

There was a kid with Down's syndrome sitting in my section today. I thought it would be nice if I could get a baseball for him. I asked Nora if she could get one for me, thinking she would simply ask one of the crowd control guys on the field to pick one up from a dugout or bullpen. (There are always some available.) She said she'd go to Customer Relations to get one for me. She never did bring one back. I was trying to go the extra mile, as we are often urged to do. Unfortunately, this car got stuck.

Final Score: Cubs 2—Brewers 1

Cubs win in the bottom of the tenth on a bases loaded walk to Jake Fox.

July 8, 2009

Kevin Hart (Cubs) versus Kenshin Kawakami (Braves)

Today Nora assigned us based on astrological signs. What will she think of next?? Oh, I know…today she came around and asked us who our favorite Cubs player is.

At our pre-game meeting today, our boss publicly wished a happy birthday to one of the ushers. Then he proceeded to announce that one of the crowd control crew is leaving to take an internship in New York. Turns out she's a singer and hoping to make it big. He presented her with a new guitar that had a picture of Wrigley embossed on it.

Final Score: Braves 4—Cubs 1

July 10, 2009

Rich Harden (Cubs) versus Chris Carpenter (Cardinals)

A fan in my section took it upon himself to walk over to two soldiers a couple of sections over and thank them for their service to our country. I saw him a while later stopping a hot dog vendor, and paying for two hot dogs.

"Please give those to the soldiers over there," he told the vendor.

Quote of the day from a kid of about five years old in the men's room as his dad took him from the urine trough to the community sink. As he was washing his hands, the kid asked: "Why do we have to share everything in here?"

Final Score: Cardinals 8—Cubs 3

July 11, 2009

Ted Lilly (Cubs) versus Brad Thompson (Cardinals)

I was asked to participate in another proposal of marriage today. The prospective groom asked me if I had ever assisted in one. Upon telling him that I had, he asked me for suggestions for the best time and place for him to pop the question. I suggested that we do it right away (this was about an hour and a half before game time) and we do it right at the wall. I asked him if he wanted me to get one of the Cubs website photographers to capture the moment. He did. So, he popped the question, and she said yes, although with surprisingly little enthusiasm. Later, they took pictures of their own and asked me to pose with them for a few.

Got a tip today—but not for wiping down seats---just for being "such a nice guy". It was from a couple from Portland, Oregon who have seven kids who are big baseball fans. They left all of them home in Portland because they "need to get away every once in a while." I'll bet.

Final Score: Cubs 5—Cardinals 2

July 24, 2009

Wrigley hosted three concerts the past week—two by Billy Joel and Elton John and one by Rascal Flatts. They've steadily increased the number of concerts each year, as it brings in mega bucks. Somehow, they deal with the issue of the toll concerts take on the field. I worked one of the two Joel/John concerts. Nothing earth-shattering took place despite the fact that there was lots of marijuana around. I heard from a few colleagues today that the Rascal Flatts concert was interesting. Apparently, the crowd was primarily made up of twenty-something females. Twenty-something females who drank A LOT of beer. Twenty-something females who didn't want to wait in the long lines at the women's restrooms and so either went to the men's rooms or decided to just let it rip, if you know what I mean.

July 25, 2009

Kevin Hart (Cubs) versus Johnny Cueto (Reds)

I am not celebrity-struck by any means. I've met several celebrities at Wrigley over the years and seen dozens of others. No great shakes. Today was a bit of an exception. Singing the seventh inning stretch was Carlos Bernard, who plays Tony on my favorite TV show, "24." He walked up my aisle after throwing out the first pitch. I shook hands with him and told him that I miss the Cubs mug he used to have at his desk on the show. He told me he was working on the producers to get it back in the show. Very nice, down-to-earth guy.

Final Score: Cubs 5—Reds 3

July 30, 2009

Kevin Hart (Cubs) versus Russ Ortiz (Astros)

Quote of the day from a fan and his buddy: Fan number one: "I'm so passionate about the Cubs, I named my two children Addison and Ryne." His friend chimed in "….and his wife's name is Harry."

Final Score: Cubs 12—Astros 3

August 9, 2009

Last year for the first time, Wrigley hosted one of the Cubs' minor league teams while the Cubs were out of town. The game was a huge draw because it featured the Cubs minor league team managed by Ryne Sandberg. Attempting to build on that success, the powers that be decided to do it again this year. No Ryne Sandberg this time. This year's game featured the Iowa Cubs, the Triple A minor league team. Today's game only drew about 15,000. It was a lot of work for those of us who worked the game. For some reason, management decided to only have a skeleton crew on hand, so there were only eleven of us on the entire left field side. On top of that, we had a lot more chasing down to do than is typical, as there were so many empty seats, and people just assumed they could sit in those seats. Furthermore, it's tougher to tell people they can't sit in those seats when so many of them are empty.

Nevertheless, it was a fun day. The game featured many of the entertainment acts that are typical in minor league games: Clowns, races, hot dogs shot into the stands, and dancing umpires. Yes, dancing umpires!

August 11, 2009

Rich Harden (Cubs) versus J.A. Happ (Phillies)

Today I was teamed up with Laverne, a first year usher who worked the cross-aisle. I asked her if she wanted to stay down by the dugout before the game while I worked the top of the aisle. She was thrilled, having never worked the lower boxes before. She told me I made her year. Laverne had a smile on her face the whole game.

Final Score: Phillies 4—Cubs 3

The Cubs tied it up in the bottom of the ninth, and lost in the twelfth.

August 12, 2009

Jeff Samardzija (Cubs) versus Pedro Martinez (Phillies)

During pre-game ceremonies today, astronaut Lee Archambault was honored. An Illinois native, he was recognized for his work in outer space and most notably, for bringing a Cubs jersey with him on the space shuttle. During the ceremony I wondered which was a bigger thrill for him— being in space or being on the field at Wrigley. I asked Dick to ask him that question if he got the chance when Mr. Archambault walked up his aisle. He did, and Archambault gave a perfectly politically correct response: "They're both so special."

Final Score: Phillies 12—Cubs 5

August 24, 2009

It started raining about 1:15; just five minutes before game time today. The grounds crew put the tarp on the field. About five minutes later, it stopped raining, but the tarp just sat there. About 2:30, the PA announced that there was a line of thunderstorms about an hour away and that we would wait for that to pass before hopefully beginning the game. In my seven years at Wrigley, I've never heard an official announcement about anticipated weather and tentative plans made. We were all very surprised. In any event, the thunderstorm never materialized. They could have started playing at 1:30 and had a good chance of getting in at least the minimum four-and-a-half innings needed to play an official game. Instead at 4:30 they officially postponed the game. A rain delay of over three hours. Needless to say, there were a lot of disappointed fans; many of whom were from out of town and won't be able to come back for the make-up game.

August 27, 2009

Randy Wells (Cubs) versus J.D. Martin (Nationals)

I've noticed several times that when Alfonso Soriano's in the on-deck circle, he pans the box seats and smiles and waves to the fans. Well...today I realized he wasn't just being a nice, friendly guy... he was cruising the women in the crowd. Louise told me he somehow gets the cell phone numbers of hot women.

Final Score: Nationals 5—Cubs 4
Soriano went 0 for 4.

August 28, 2009

Ted Lilly (Cubs) versus Pat Misch (Mets)

I've been offered bribes for better seats several times... but today might have taken the cake. Two boys who couldn't have been more than fourteen years old showed me their tickets. They were for the upper deck. A five dollar bill was folded in between the two tickets. It was tough keeping a straight face when I told them that I couldn't do anything for them.

Final Score: Cubs 5—Mets 2

August 30, 2009

Carlos Zambrano (Cubs) versus Nelson Figueroa (Mets)

Quote of the day from a fan who, as he showed me his tickets to determine where his seats were said, "Am I in the ballpark?"

Final Score: Mets 4—Cubs 1

September 16, 2009

Rich Harden (Cubs) versus Braden Looper (Brewers)

Quote of the day from one of the Cubs ground crew when asked by a Milwaukee Brewers fan during batting practice where Prince Fielder is: "Probably eating." (in reference to Prince's semi-obese build.)

Final Score: Brewers 9—Cubs 5

September 17, 2009

Randy Wells (Cubs) versus David Bush (Brewers)

Today they didn't have any chamois, and instead gave us really cheap and useless towelette-type rags. I guess the lousy economy is taking its toll on everyone.

Final Score: Brewers 7—Cubs 4

October 2, 2009

Tom Gorzelanny (Cubs) versus Billy Buckner (Diamondbacks)

Something happened today that I've never seen before. Two beer vendors approached my aisle at the same time. Usually when that happens, one graciously lets the other take the aisle. But today, one shoved the other out of the way. A minor verbal and physical scuffle ensued. The shovee lost the battle. He commented to me that the other guy does this all the time, although I've never seen him do it. Like I said, the economy is affecting everyone.

Sight seen—two guys sitting in the first row behind home plate dressed in major league home plate umpire outfits—the full costume—including masks, chest protectors, etc. They were calling balls and strikes, plays at the plate, etc.

Pretty funny.

Final Score: Diamondbacks 12—Cubs 3

October 3, 2009

Randy Wells (Cubs) versus Daniel Cabrera (Diamond-backs)

Randy Wells, a rookie pitcher was throwing a great game today. He had quite a few strike outs, and I was trying to find out how many. Nobody has been posting "K's" at the building across the street from the left field bleachers this year, as has been the custom the last few years. So I started looking around for someone who was keeping score. Couldn't find anyone in my whole section that had a scorecard! I realized something that I guess I had been subconsciously aware of—very few people keep score these days. It could be because so few people are really into the game, or it could be because people don't know how to any more—computers do everything like that now.

Today must have been "no teeth day." I saw three guys in the stands who were missing at least one tooth. I'm sure it's coincidental that it's the end of a lousy year and season ticket holders are pretty much giving their tickets away. Perhaps even to homeless, toothless guys.

Quote of the day—from a kid about ten years old who was craving autographs before the game. He yelled out to Reed Johnson who was approaching the wall where the kid was standing: "Reed, you're my second favorite player."

Lots of laughs from the fans in the area.

Final Score: Cubs 5—Diamondbacks 0

Randy Wells had ten strikeouts, by the way.

October 4, 2009

Ryan Dempster (Cubs) versus Doug Davis (Diamond-backs)

Today marked the last day of what turned out to be a very disappointing season for the team. It was bittersweet—good to get this lousy season behind us, but sad to say goodbye to my friends. Hopefully, I'll see many of them at the end of year party.

It figures; the last game of the season, and I get a trouble-maker in my section. Toward the middle of the game, this guy started yelling at the ballplayers, cheering for them very loudly. He was very annoying to me and the fans around him, but he was not using foul language and wasn't drunk, so there was really nothing I could do. I did go up to him to ask him if he could take it down a notch. He gave me a bit of an argument. A woman sitting close to me empathized; saying that she knew my hands were tied. The guy left the game in the eighth inning. At that point, the woman complimented me on how well I handled the situation. She said, "You practically need a degree in psychology (which I have) to do this job."

How appropriate that hers was the last comment of the season.

Final Score: Diamondbacks 5—Cubs 2

Cubs in second place, seven and a half games behind the Cardinals.

THE EIGHTH INNING—
THE 2010 SEASON

```
TEAM RECORD: 75-87
STANDING: 5TH PLACE
MANAGER: LOU PINIELLA/MIKE QUADE
ATTENDANCE: 3,062,973
```

April 12, 2010

Ryan Dempster (Cubs) versus Doug Davis (Brewers)

Another Opening Day. Today was probably the nicest weather on Opening Day since I've been working. It was about sixty-two degrees. The forecast is for seventies the rest of the week.

This year marks the beginning of a new regime—the Ricketts family took over as owners during the off-season. They've made a lot of aesthetic changes to the ballpark— modernized a couple of the bathrooms, enhanced the food service (including the addition of bison to the menu, as the senior Ricketts owns a Buffalo ranch). They've also added a couple of advertising signs in the park. As a Wrigley purist, I abhor advertising of any type in the park, but I guess you gotta pay those players' salaries.

A new employee group has been added this year: "Cubs Ambassadors". These are people who roam the park and help out fans by answering their questions, giving Cubs stickers to kids, etc. Supposedly, the ambassadors will also be roaming outside the park, answering emails and phone calls, etc. It's an idea that has worked well, first in Boston, and then in Los Angeles. We'll see how it works here. It's interesting that they hired about twenty-five people, twenty-three of whom seem to be under the age of twenty-five.

Unfortunately, the Ricketts haven't done much to improve the product on the field. I have a feeling it's going to be a very long year.

Four of the "seniorest" ushers have retired. Luellen, Esther, Lenore, and Jed have turned in their chamois. Luellen and Esther were both going to turn ninety-four or ninety-five this year and Jed had to be at least ninety. Lenore was the baby of the group; she was probably only eighty or so, and the word is that she is quite ill. I had a feeling Luellen would retire, and Jed had told me he was going to. But Esther was a surprise. She did show up today as a fan. She said she decided a few weeks ago that it's time to hang it up. I'll miss them all. Wonder if Luellen will miss me. Randy, who's always kidded me about Luellen and me having a thing, said he hopes I don't take her absence too hard.

Final Score: Cubs 9—Brewers 5

April 15, 2010

Carlos Zambrano (Cubs) versus Jeff Suppan (Brewers)
Because the weather was so great this week, I added today's game to my schedule. (I also added this Saturday).

Shortly after I received my assignment, Brian asked me if I'd go help out with scanning tickets at Gate F. The Cubs introduced scanners to process tickets a couple of seasons ago. (I believe they are the last team in the major leagues to make use of this technology.) Since I'd never scanned before, it took me a while to get the hang of it, and I had to ask for help from a couple of the kids a few times. As time went on, it got easier, although I never totally mastered the science of it. About an hour into it, my wrist started hurting like crazy due to the repetitiveness of the work. I was glad when I was sent back to the mezzanine about forty minutes after the game started. As Adam, the supervisor at the gate signed me out, he told me he was giving me an "AA" recommendation because I was so cooperative with learning my new role. "AA" is a new part of the recently revised evaluation system. It stands for Associate of the Area (we've been called "associates" since the Ricketts took over). It's worth five points, for what it's worth. Nice of Adam.

I was asked to be the break usher for all of the upper deck ushers to the right of home plate. I hadn't worked the upper deck since my first year. It certainly is a different experience up there. Many people like the panoramic view it offers. Others feel it provides a more relaxed atmosphere to watch a game. I was reminded that for at least a couple of decades the upper deck wasn't even open on week days. Attendance was so poor for so many of the Wrigley family ownership years, that it didn't make sense to keep that part of the park open. Back then, I never gave it a second thought. Now, as an employee, I realize it must have been an economic decision. Boy, times have changed.

I finished my usher-break duties and returned to my original assignment. It's the first time I spent the entire day on my feet in a very long time. My feet ached like crazy.

Final Score: Brewers 8—Cubs 6

April 17, 2010

Tom Gorzelanny (Cubs) versus Roy Oswalt (Astros)

Back to typical April weather---not bad in the sun, but very cold in the shade. I was assigned to Aisle 101, which for a significant part of the day was the only place on the left field side that had any sun. As a result, scores of people wanted to sit in empty seats in my section. (Next time it's fifty-five degrees, wear something more than a t-shirt.) I was chasing people away all day. Early in the game, one fan told me he was going to count how many people I had to shoo away, and that my goal should be a hundred. I asked him if I get bonus points for getting rid of people who offered me a bribe. (One guy showed me a $20.)

Final Score: Astros 4—Cubs 3

April 18, 2010

Ryan Dempster (Cubs) versus Wandy Rodriguez (Astros)

Unlikely event of the day: A fan in my section caught a ball that the third base coach tossed to him. On the very next pitch, the same guy caught a foul ball that bounced down from the upper deck.

Final Score: Astros 3—Cubs 2

April 28, 2010

Ryan Dempster (Cubs) versus Luis Atilano (Nationals)

I worked Aisle 16 in Sally's absence today, so I saw a lot of the Ricketts Family. Both Tom and Todd Ricketts were there a lot, and both are very friendly and personable. Todd introduced himself to me, while Tom was very busy signing autographs for the throngs that approached him. One vendor quipped that Tom is like the Jesus of Wrigley.

Final Score: Nationals 3—Cubs 2

April 29, 2010

Ted Lilly (Cubs) versus Ian Kennedy (Diamondbacks)
Spent some time before the game talking with a photographer from Topps, the baseball card company. He's taken pictures for them for a number of years and has been at every major league ballpark. When I asked him what his favorite park was, he said Wrigley and Fenway. No surprise.

Final Score: Diamondbacks 13—Cubs 5

May 1, 2010

Carlos Silva (Cubs) versus Dan Haren (Diamondbacks)
Another beautiful day in what has been the nicest early season weather-wise since I started. But, oh, no! Fans did the Wave today. As I've mentioned, over the years, there have been feeble attempts to do the Wave, but they've never been very successful. Today's effort was, though. The Wave circled the stadium (including the bleachers) at least three times. Let's hope this is not the start of something. Wrigley has always prided itself on not having to stoop to what I call "boredom reduction activities."

Final Score: Cubs 7—Diamondbacks 5

Derrek Lee knocked in the game winning runs in the bottom of the eighth.

May 2, 2010

Tom Gorzelanny (Cubs) versus Edwin Jackson (Diamondbacks)

One of the new activities that has been initiated this year is a youngster announcing "play ball" on the PA system at the start of the game on Sundays. A nice added touch, I think. I happened to see today's guest announcer on his way to the booth. He looked as if he was on his way to have a root canal. His father, on the other hand, had a huge smile on his face.

Final Score: Cubs 10—Diamondbacks 5

May 18, 2010

Carlos Silva (Cubs) versus Jhoulis Chacin (Rockies)

I sat Ron Howard today, although I didn't realize it until later. He was quite incognito---baseball cap, dark shades, etc. Although I checked periodically, it was tough to tell if he was rooting for the Cubs. Come on, Opie!

Final Score: Cubs 6—Rockies 2

May 26, 2010

Tom Gorzelanny (Cubs) versus Chad Billingsley (Dodgers)

Tonight the lights went out at Wrigley. It was about 8:15 and almost completely dark. The auxiliary lights came right back on, but it takes the field lights about fifteen minutes to come back. It was eerie. For a few minutes all you could see were flashbulbs going off. People kept asking if this was the

first time this ever happened. All of the ushers agreed that it was, although the media claims that it happened twice in 2003. None of us remember that. Sign of the day appeared the next day on the marquee at Murphy's, the bar across the street from Wrigley. It read: "Day baseball; no lights needed."
Final Score: Dodgers 8—Cubs 5

May 27, 2010
Ted Lilly (Cubs) versus John Ely (Dodgers)
A woman who was sitting a couple of rows above me kept coming down to straighten my ID lanyard. It really bothered her that it didn't lay straight. She said she has season tickets and will be checking me out every game that I work her section.
Final Score: Cubs 1—Dodgers 0
Tyler Colvin knocked in the game's only run in the eighth.

May 30, 2010
Ryan Dempster (Cubs) versus Adam Wainwright (Cardinals)
A young couple from Nashville whom I took a picture of last year as the young man proposed to his girl friend came up to me after today's game. They found me to thank me for taking pictures last year. They said they've been showing the picture of the three of us to everyone they know since they were here last year.
Final Score: Cardinals 9—Cubs 1

June 11, 2010
Randy Wells (Cubs) versus Jake Peavy (White Sox)

Today is the first day the Cubs have played since they erected a big Toyota sign in the left field bleachers. Ugh! I suppose it could have been worse, but it's not inconspicuous by any means. Traditionalist that I am, it saddens me greatly to see any change at the ballpark that takes away from its charm.

And speaking of change, as each Cub approached home plate today, Gary Pressy, the organist played a recording of rock music (a different song for each player). They do this at a lot of stadiums, but it seems out of place at Wrigley. For years, Pressy played "cutesy" songs for each Cub. That is so much more in line with the charm of this place.

A celebration to honor the Blackhawks who won the Stanley Cup this week was held downtown today. Chicago, of course, has gone crazy for the Hawks, and there were rumors that they would be bringing the Cup to the park. That didn't happen. What did happen, though, was that the start time of the game was delayed twenty minutes because so many people had been downtown at the Blackhawks rally, and they all arrived at Wrigley right before game time. Apparently, the gates were a mob scene, so someone decided to delay the game. That's the first time I know of that this has been done.

A guy approached me today to tell me that he was an Andy Frain usher in 1968 and 1969. Andy Frain was the company that the Cubs employed to provide security in those days. Who could forget their dark blue pants, jackets and caps, all distinctly trimmed with gold piping, the crisp white shirts and gold ties? They looked like they were dressed for a president's funeral; not a baseball game. (Of course, in those days, many of the fans were pretty formal, too—men in coats and ties and women in fancy dresses.) Andy Frain ushers were feared by many a youngster, so to try to get by them was a bold endeavor. The gentleman who stopped me today told me that he got paid seven dollars per game and a free burger at Bernie's if he was in uniform. It must have been a blast during the '69 season when the Cubs blew the pennant.

By the way, I can't believe the number of times that I've been referred to as an "Andy Frain usher." Fans do it when they are talking to me at the park ("How do you like your job as an Andy Frain usher?"). Friends do it, as well. ("Meet my friend Bruce; he's an Andy Frain usher at Wrigley Field."). It's been decades since the Andy Frain Company worked at Wrigley. Perhaps it's symbolic of our need to hang on to those good old days.

Final Score: White Sox 10—Cubs 5

June 13, 2010

Ted Lilly (Cubs) versus Gavin Floyd (White Sox)

What a night! The World Champion Chicago Black-hawks were at Wrigley. Ceremonies began about a half-hour before game time with the Hawks parading around the entire field with the Stanley Cup raised above their heads. All the while, their theme song was playing. Then the Cubs, White Sox (the Cubs played the White Sox today) and Hawks all posed on the field for pictures. Later on, the Hawks were the guest singers for the seventh inning stretch. How poignant it was to see ESPN announcers John Miller and Joe Morgan taking their own personal pictures of the

Hawks as they sang.

And then….what a game. Both the White Sox pitcher and Ted Lilly of the Cubs threw no-hitters into the seventh inning. The Cubs broke through for a run in the seventh. It started raining in the eighth, so everyone was crossing their fingers that the umps wouldn't call the game. They didn't, and Lilly pitched a perfect eighth. But he did give up a hit to the first man he faced in the ninth. He was then taken out of the game (to a standing ovation, of course), and the Cubs held on to win.

Final Score: Cubs 1—White Sox 0

June 16, 2010

Ryan Dempster (Cubs) versus Gio Gonzalez (A's)

Word came today that Vern passed away yesterday. I'll truly miss him—he was a great guy. This news came on top of hearing that Lenore passed away a couple of weeks ago. I have fond memories of her, as well. Working with this older demographic certainly can have its disadvantages.

Final Score: Cubs 6—A's 2

June 19, 2010

Ted Lilly (Cubs) versus Jered Weaver (Angels)

A fan asked me if the net behind home plate was made of vinyl or mesh. I've had some obscure questions before, but this one took the cake. I told him I had no idea and suggested he go down and check it out. He touched it for a fraction of a second and came back to report that it is nylon.

Today was one of the first really warm days of the year. As I was applying sunscreen, a fan asked me if he could use some. Before I knew it, four or five people asked to use some. Quote of the day came from the last guy to use it who thought he accidentally swallowed some--- "at least I know my guts won't get sunburn."

Final Score: Angels 12—Cubs 0

June 28, 2010

Randy Wells (Cubs) versus Paul Maholm (Pirates)

Just after the national anthem was sung, I saw one of the vendors run over to the left field foul pole. He proceeded to mumble a few words to himself, kiss the foul pole, and then point to the sky. I asked him what he was doing, and he replied that it was a superstitious ritual, and he's been doing it for a long time. Too bad it's not working.

Final Score: Pirates 2—Cubs 1

June 30, 2010

Tom Gorzelanny (Cubs) versus Brad Lincoln (Pirates)

A very warm day today with a cloudless blue sky. All of a sudden, for just a moment, the sun went away---what happened?? A blimp that had been circling the park for a couple of hours flew between the sun and the field. A huge cheer rang out from the crowd.

Final Score: Pirates 2—Cubs 0

July 7, 2010

Tonight featured this year's minor league game. It was the Cubs franchise, Peoria Chiefs against the Kane County Cougars. Like last year, it was a small crowd and there was a skeleton crew to work the game. There was plenty of between-inning entertainment featuring the famous Chicken. Oh, and $3.50 beers in the bleachers. We were told we could send people from the grandstand to the bleachers if they asked, (something that is not allowed during regular games) as beers in the grandstand were $6.75. The logic of this escapes me.

Much of today's crowd was composed of families. One family I talked to had managed to drag their seven year old son, who is a diehard White Sox fan, to the game. He had heretofore refused to step in Wrigley Field, but consented today when his parents told him the Cubs wouldn't be there.

Indeed, many other families were enjoying their first outing at Wrigley, probably because of the significantly cheaper ticket cost. One mother, upon asking the price of popcorn, asked the vendor if he took debit cards. I guess novices don't realize how expensive a game at the ballpark can be.

July 16, 2010

Ted Lilly (Cubs) versus Joe Blanton (Phillies)

A hot day today. Somebody (I was told it was Ralph, who by the way, became an assistant to James last year) had the great idea that on hot days, those of us in the lower boxes should get to trade places with another usher up in the grandstand for five or ten minutes to get out of the sun. Great idea! Why did it take them all these years to figure that out?

Quote of the day: I asked a fan if he and the people he was standing with were all together. His response: "Only some of the time."

Final Score: Cubs 4—Phillies 3

Aramis Ramirez homered in the bottom of the eighth to win it.

July 18, 2010

Tom Gorzelanny (Cubs) versus Roy Halladay (Phillies)
Sight seen today---man drinking beer with a straw.
Final Score: Cubs 11—Phillies 6

July 19, 2010

Carlos Silva (Cubs) versus Wandy Rodriguez (Astros)
A new usher, Bryce, told me today that he has spent most of this first year in the upper deck or the mezzanine. He told me Maury was his supervisor up there.

"One time, I made a humorous comment about a fan who didn't have very many teeth," Bryce explained, "And Maury couldn't stop laughing. He gave me the AA award that day because I was so funny."

Now THAT'S a good reason to earn the associate of the area award.

Final Score: Astros 11—Cubs 5

July 21, 2010

Ted Lilly (Cubs) versus Brett Myers (Astros)
Quote of the day on this very hot day from a fan who gleefully noted "the hotter it gets, the more the girls take off."

Or should this be quote of the day? From a kid I kicked out of his seat in the tenth inning: "I don't understand; nobody paid for this seat for more than nine innings."

Final Score: Astros 4—Cubs 3 (twelve innings)

The score was tied 1-1 after nine.

July 23, 2010

Randy Wells (Cubs) versus Jeff Suppan (Cardinals)

Today was the hottest day of the year, getting up into the mid-nineties. Someone had a bright idea: passing out wet, cold towels for us. They helped immensely. Another idea that should have been hatched a long time ago.

I met a fan today who claimed his name is Roger Hornsby, the name of the famous Cub. I told him I didn't believe him, but he showed me his ID. Sure enough. He said his father's name was Rogers (with the "s") and his grandmother named him that because she was a huge Rogers Hornsby fan.

Final Score: Cubs 5—Cardinals 0

July 25, 2010

Ryan Dempster (Cubs) versus Chris Carpenter (Cardinals)

I had one of my more interesting encounters with a fan today. A Cardinals fan was standing to take a picture of Albert Pujols.

"Please sit down," I said.

"I will in a minute," she replied.

"Please do it now," I asked. "You're blocking the view for everyone else."

She did, but made no attempt to hide her feelings about me. A minute later when I looked back at her (right after Pujols hit a home run), she gave me the finger. Then she and her husband started going off at me, telling me to mind my own business and tend to more serious problems. I "wrote it up" (as we are supposed to do when an incident like this occurs) and gave the report to Carmella. A moment later, Carmella escorted the woman away. Before they left the game, the husband made sure to come down to tell me in no uncertain terms what he thought of me and the "so called friendly confines." I can't wait to find out from Carmella what she told them.

Final Score: Cardinals 4—Cubs 3 (eleven innings)

August 2, 2010

Randy Wells (Cubs) versus Yovani Gallardo (Brewers)

Today we learned that Esther passed away. She suffered an aneurysm a couple of weeks ago. What a great woman she was. She will be sorely missed by ushers and her devoted "customers" as well. Her legacy lives on though, as Adam, the supervisor, is her son.

The Cubs got clobbered by the Brewers today. Here's an interesting tidbit: Astute Cubs fans may know that the scoreboard displays the number of hits each team has in yellow numbers. Well...apparently the highest yellow number they have in stock is 25. The Brewers got 26 hits (yikes!) and number 26 went up in white. Hope we never have to see that again.

Final Score: Brewers 18—Cubs 1

August 6, 2010

Tom Gorzelanny (Cubs) versus Bronson Arroyo (Reds)

The guest speaker at our meeting today was the new VP of Marketing. He mentioned that on average, close to forty percent of those who attend Cubs games come from outside of Illinois. I knew the percentage would be high, but I didn't think that high. That's impressive. I've been told several times that Wrigley Field is the third largest tourist attraction in Chicago (behind Navy Pier and Sears Tower), so it all adds up.

Final Score: Reds 3—Cubs 0

August 8, 2010

Thomas Diamond (Cubs) versus Travis Wood (Reds)

Quote of the day from a White Sox fan as I was wiping down her rain-soaked seat: "Now THAT'S something you don't see at Sox Park."

Final Score: Reds 11—Cubs 4

August 18, 2010

Casey Coleman (Cubs) versus Clayton Richard (Padres)

The poor economy and the Cubs horrendous season continue to take its toll on attendance. Today's attendance was announced as 33,000 plus. A far cry from the full houses we're used to seeing. The crowds have been smaller for several weeks now. Makes for a totally different atmosphere at the park.

Final Score: Padres 5—Cubs 1

August 30, 2010

Carlos Zambrano (Cubs) versus Paul Maholm (Pirates)

Today was Andre Dawson Day. The Cubs honored him in conjunction with his induction into the Hall of Fame earlier this year. Too bad they waited until this late in the season, as there were relatively few people there to witness the festivities. At the start of the game there were only twenty-six people in my section that holds over a hundred and twenty people.

Final Score: Cubs 14—Pirates 2

September 1, 2010

Tom Gorzelanny (Cubs) versus James McDonald (Pirates)
Talked to a fan who hadn't been at Wrigley for sixty-two years. He was jubilant; had tears in his eyes.

Final Score: Cubs 5—Pirates 3

September 3, 2010

Randy Wells (Cubs) versus R.A. Dickey (Mets)
There were a half dozen dark suited secret-service types hanging around my stairway. Usually, there are one or two bodyguards when someone "important" is in the house. Everyone was curious, fans and employees alike. Word from James was that it was just a test; that no celebrity or political figure was in attendance. All of them were wearing a yellow triangle on their lapel. I asked one of them what it signified, and he gave a very coy response of, "so we can identify each other." At least he didn't say that if he told me, he'd have to kill me.

Final Score: Cubs 7—Mets 6

September 8, 2010

Our boss announced on Monday that the Ricketts were hosting an "associate recognition" event at noon today. We were all invited to attend, but it was not mandatory. He didn't say much more other than pizza would be provided.

Although I wasn't scheduled to work the night game tonight, I decided to satisfy my curiosity and find out what it was all about, so I drove down to attend the gig. As we arrived, we were directed to sit in the box seats directly behind home plate. Those of us sitting in the first couple of rows were asked to sign a release. Many of us inferred that we were going to be videoed. Then we were taken out on the field surrounding home plate where Tom Ricketts thanked us for a great year and then introduced his brother Todd. Todd announced that he had gone undercover the last week or so while filming an episode of CBS' *Undercover Boss*. Apparently, the last segment of that show features employees discovering that their boss had gone undercover, so they needed to film us making this discovery. We were filling a need, so the "appreciation" event turned out to be somewhat of a ruse, but, that's OK; it was fun to go out on the field and watch footage of what Todd had done. Much of it was quite comical. The show will air in October or November. Oh, and the pizza was from Connie's and was quite good. They also gave us one of the giveaways from a few weeks ago--a key chain filled with Wrigley Field dirt. The drive in was definitely worth it. Wonder if I'll be on the show, or if I'll wind up on the cutting room floor.

September 22, 2010
Randy Wells (Cubs) versus Jonathan Sanchez (Giants)

Quote of the day when I asked a fan if he needed help finding his seat: "Well, yes, I either need you or a GPS."

Found out in the locker room that one of the first-year ushers has been journaling his daily experiences at the park.

Uh-oh. Do I need to worry about competition?

Final Score: Cubs 2—Giants 0

September 26, 2010

Jeff Samardzija (Cubs) versus Jake Westbrook (Cardinals)

Today was the last day of my eighth season. A truly forgettable season on the field, as the Cubs underachieved from day one and will probably wind up in fifth place. On the other hand, it was not entirely a "downer" season. Changes that the new-owner-Ricketts family implemented proved to be positive for the most part. Much of what they've done is fan-driven. For example, today before game time, all of the Cubs came out on the field and threw out baseballs to the fans in the stands. Little touches like that can go a long way—hopefully, long enough to soothe the fans' anger at their on-field performance.

An interesting side note to this year's archive: it didn't rain at any game that I worked the entire year for more than a few minutes. I never wore a poncho for more than five minutes all year. That's always a positive!

Final Score: Cardinals 8—Cubs 7

October 5, 2010

Today was the end of the year party. It was preceded by a feedback forum that we were invited to attend. The forum was held in the beautiful sunshine of the left field bullpen box seats

A lot of topics were discussed, and our boss actually did take notes on a couple of things including my suggestion that he needs to do a better job of communicating day to day operational matters such as the rule change that was made about people being permitted to put things on the wall prior to game time. All in all, it was, I thought, an effective meeting.

Immediately after, we walked over to John Barleycorn for the party. This is the second consecutive year the party has been there--it is a much better venue than Slugger's where it had been held previously. As usual, it was good to talk and say goodbye to all my buddies. Tom Ricketts showed up, as did Mike Quade, the current manager. Caroline, who knows Quade from his Mount Prospect days, introduced me to him. He was very friendly and down-to-earth.

THE NINTH INNING– THE 2011 SEASON

The year started a bit differently, as I did not work the convention. When I realized about ten days before the convention that I hadn't heard anything about working, I called the office. I was told that people like me who had only signed up to work one of the three days of the event were not hired to work the convention. I know that convention attendance was down this year (for the first time in many years—a foreshadowing of things to come this summer?), so they probably needed fewer of us and decided to go with people willing to work more hours.

March 26, 2011

This year's Part Two of training took place in the usual below freezing temperatures. That's bad enough, but we spent no more than twenty-five minutes of the four hour session learning anything. The rest of the time was spent standing around talking with each other while shivering to death. I'm beginning to think that the end of the line is near for me.

They did provide us with a better than ever lunch, though. This year, instead of the usual hot dogs (which I never eat because they're not kosher style—yuck), they had several other items. Figures-- for the first time, thinking ahead about the horrendous hot dogs, I brought a lunch from home. I sampled a pizza which was good. This year they're switching from Connie's pizza to DiAgostino's and from the yucky hot dogs to Vienna. This could portend trouble for my cholesterol levels this summer—I like both of those items; it will be hard to avoid them.

Rose told me that Louise is not returning this year. Apparently, Louise says it's never been the same since Oliver, her husband passed away a few years ago.

April 1, 2011

Ryan Dempster (Cubs) versus Kevin Correia (Pirates)

Opening Day. All the rain I missed last year must have been stored up and delivered today. It started just before the game and didn't stop until the eighth inning. It was a light rain the whole time, so the game was never delayed, but it was raw, and by the time it was over, my feet were soaked.

Our boss announced during our pre-game meeting that they had designed a new form that gives up to the minute info that they will distribute to us prior to each game (or maybe each new home stand, I'm not sure). In any event, I think this might be a result of the suggestion I made last year.

Pre-game activities included a moment of silence for Ron Santo who passed away during the off-season. All players will wear the number 10 on their uniform sleeve in his honor this season, and our caps have a number 10 sewn on them. There will be a Ron Santo day in August. A fan showed me his Cubs jacket that had Santo's name written on the inside collar. He told me it was his father's jacket from the 1969 season; that his father did some work at Santo's house and Santo gave it to him in the early seventies. We hear lots of these types of fantasies, but I have a hunch this one was true.

I worked by the media/photo box next to the Cubs dugout. Local sportscaster Rafer Wiegel, son of well-known Chicago sportscaster Tim Weigel, walked past me, and I congratulated him on his recent hiring at Channel 7. He thanked me and told me how excited he was to be at Wrigley Field. He said it was his first time on the field since he was a young kid and his dad brought him there. He's a very genuine, likeable guy.

Final Score: Pirates 6—Cubs 3

April 21, 2011

It is with mixed emotions that I proclaim that as of today, April 21, 2011 I am no longer an employee of the Chicago Cubs.

Let me explain. During the past couple of years, as the price of gas has gone up, I've toyed with the idea of quitting. I calculated the other day that if I subtract the price of gas from a typical day's salary this year, I net about $25 or $30 per day. Add to that the wear and tear on my car, especially the dings and nicks on my rear bumper from all of the parallel parking, and I come out a pretty big loser financially.

I've known this for a long time now, but somehow always decided to stick with it because I loved being at the games, enjoyed the friendship of my colleagues and relished the opportunity to share Cubs and Wrigley enthusiasm with fans from all over the world. I figured the transportation cost was a small price to pay, so I kept on coming to games. Until today.

About a week ago I received a letter in the mail from my boss' office. The letter was accompanied by a copy of the test I turned in at training last month. (The test we are given to take home at each year's March training session.) The test includes a few "short answer" questions. As I've done the past several years, I typed my answers to these questions on my computer, printed them out, and taped them in the appropriate space on the test paper. I do this because I type much faster than I write, because my hand hurts when I write for any length of time, and, perhaps most importantly, because nobody can read my writing.

The letter advised me that I could not simply cut the answers from the Cubs Handbook and paste them on the test paper; that I must answer the questions in my own words. I was amused by what seemed like an admonishment from my third grade teacher. I called the next day to explain that my answers were not cut from the Cubs Handbook; that they were, indeed, in my own words; that I simply type these words rather than write them. I was told that they would not accept typed answers; that they have to be written. I needed to resubmit the *entire* test (the short answers comprise only about ten percent of the test) and complete it in pen, not pencil.

I thought I'd give it a day or two to cool off before I made a decision about what to do. At first I decided that I should just play the game. After all, if I didn't do what they wanted, I would have to give up what so many people have told me is the "greatest job in the world." I started to redo the test. But after a few minutes, I just couldn't do it. It was ludicrous. I left a voicemail to ask if there was some compromise we could come to. I didn't get a call back.

And so I decided it might be time to leave. This was not an easy decision. As I mentioned earlier, this was something that I'd been thinking about for a while. I knew there were many reasons to stay---all the things I love about the job. And I must admit, I also thought, "What if, oh my God, what if this is the year the Cubs finally go all the way?" But I also knew the writing was on the wall (although not typed).

So today I called to say I was resigning. I didn't say why. I said that my other part-time jobs were going to demand more of my time (which is true), so I wouldn't be able to work very many games. They were actually very gracious. I said how much I had enjoyed my time at Wrigley. I was told that I was valued as an employee and that if I was interested in returning next year I should give them a call. They also asked me to put my decision in writing.

I think that's when I realized it might behoove me to word my letter not as one of resignation, but one of a leave of absence. After all, what if I am really unhappy about my decision in a few months? What if, despite it all, I really miss this job? Resignation is so final. So I told them in my letter that I was looking for a leave of absence. That leaves the door open for me to return, if not later this year, then next.

Because you never know. Maybe the Cubs WILL go all the way.

If I never make it back, here is my final record as an usher…

Year	W	L
2003	19	25
2004	23	17
2005	20	21
2006	14	32
2007	25	24
2008	37	16
2009	28	18
2010	24	25
2011	0	1
Total	190	179

EXTRA INNINGS

It's been a while now since I turned in my resignation papers. Since I've been gone, I've been spending more than a little time reflecting upon my tenure as a Cubs usher, most often when I'm watching a game on TV. I find it interesting that while watching, I'm more focused on seeing which ushers are working that game and wondering how they're doing than I am on the game itself. Of course, the way the Cubs have been playing this year (2014), that's not all that difficult.

During one of the first games I watched, I recalled that as a kid, I had never thought about becoming a Cubs usher. In fact, I never gave it a thought until the year before I retired from my job as a college administrator. It's not like I had a lifelong dream of being an usher at Wrigley Field. No, my career in crowd control didn't begin until 2002 when I was sitting in the grandstand and happened to notice an usher guarding an aisle behind third base. Out of nowhere the thought occurred to me that as a retiree (I was going to be retiring the following year) I might be able get such a job. How much fun would that be? Every Cubs fan in the world would want that job. It couldn't hurt to ask the usher about the possibilities and procedures for taking his job from him.

I said something like, "I bet it's really tough to get this job." (In my years working as an usher, I can't count the number of times people have uttered those very same words to me.) He replied that he didn't think it was out of the question; that I should call the Cubs late in the fall to find out whether they were planning on adding staff for the following season. I made a mental note to do so, thanked him for his time and went back to my seat, rather exhilarated that maybe I'd be working at Wrigley in a year. The rest is history.

As I watched games on television, I also found myself remembering some of the sights and sounds of Wrigley from my younger days. Looking for and sometimes chasing down the Smoky Links cart as it traversed the walkway between the box seats and grandstand. Listening to Pat Pieper telling us to get our pencils and scorecards ready so that he could give us the correct starting lineups for the day's game. How relatively inexpensive it was to go to a game until the recent past.

I also have thought back to some of the special games I attended as a fan throughout the years. For example, the 1962 All-Star game when my cousin and I decided at 10:00 that morning it would be cool to go, so we hopped on a bus and got bleacher seats (Boy, times have changed!) I was also there for Ernie Banks Day when they honored my favorite Cub, and I witnessed the first complete night game in August, 1988. I really enjoyed sharing the joy and misery with Jack Brickhouse and Harry Caray while I watched from my living room. I'd listen to Jack yelling "Hey,Hey" when the Cubs homered, and "Cmoooooon Ernie" when Banks was at the plate. And who could forget listening to Harry Caray engage the crowd every seventh inning with his special rendition of "Take Me Out to the Ballgame."

I've spent time, too, thinking about how Wrigley Field
has been such an important part of my life and I'm sure, part
of the lives of millions of others. Wrigley provides something
that very few things in life can provide-- a sense of comfort
and stability. For with all the change the world goes through;
the good, the bad, the craziness, Wrigley Field is a constant. Wrigley Field is still Wrigley Field. Sure, things change
there; lights are added, ads are placed in the park, prices
increase, bathrooms are modernized. There may be different
players, different front-office personnel, or different vendors,
but Wrigley Field is still Wrigley Field.

And finally, I think about how fortunate I have been
to experience this magical place from both the inside and
outside. As a fan, I attended games for over fifty years…
games I would sneak down to the box seats with my school
buddies… games I would eat three or four hot dogs because
I was with my parents and all the food was on them… games
that I took my son to when he was a youngster and he would
ask me to buy every souvenir he set his eyes on, and when he
was older and we would analyze every play of the game.

And then as an usher, I was in a position to experience
my team from within…to walk the stairways to heaven of
this most sacred of major league ballparks… to be able share
my enthusiasm and passion for the Cubs with that of Cubs
fans from all over the world, and share my love of Chicago
with tourists who wanted to know where to eat or what
Chi-town attractions to visit. But, perhaps most importantly,
it gave me the opportunity to work with some of the finest
people I've had ever had the pleasure of knowing. Sure, we
all had our love for the Cubs in common, but beyond that,

this group was comprised of truly good souls; people anyone would be proud to know.

It's been a great run; one that I wouldn't trade for anything in the world. Thank you, Chicago Cubs for giving me the opportunity to have what so many have told me is the best job in the world. Thank you, Chicago Cubs for giving me the best seat in the house.

ACKNOWLEDGMENTS

To Rochelle, whose constant encouragement and literary wherewithal served as the impetus for getting this project off the ground. To her friend, Sue who helped me edit the all-important first draft. To Victor, whose creative genius imagined this book's wonderful cover. To my brother David, who provided such valuable advice. To Rick, whose support for this project made it happen. To my fellow ushers whose dedication to and passion for the Cubs is remarkable and who made my time with the Cubs organization a truly wonderful experience. To my friends and family who exclaimed "You're writing a book about it…what a great idea!" Hopefully, they were right.

And to my son, Jason…

After "mommy" and "daddy," my son, Jason's first words were "Go Cubs." Yes, I'm guilty of instilling in him at a very young age the devotion to a team that had never won a World Series in my lifetime and who, I'm afraid may never win one in his. I took Jason to his first Cubs game at Wrigley Field in 1980 when he was three-and-a-half years old. I remember hoping that he would make it through four or five innings. To my surprise, he made it through the entire game, mesmerized by both the activity on the field and in the stands. He was hooked!

Since then, Jason and I have shared a little jubilation and a lot of misery over our Cubs. Though much of that time has been spent commiserating, it has been time that I wouldn't trade for anything; time that has provided us with invaluable bonding opportunities. It's been a wonderful ride!

ABOUT THE AUTHOR

BRUCE BOHRER was born and raised on the North Side of Chicago where he became an avid Cubs fan. He attended his first game at Wrigley Field at a very young age. Having spent most of his life in the Chicago area, he has witnessed hundreds of games at Wrigley, first as a fan, and then as an usher. "Best Seat in the House: Diary of a Wrigley Field Usher" is his first book.

Bruce with his granddaughter Lucy, a future Cubs fan, no doubt about it!

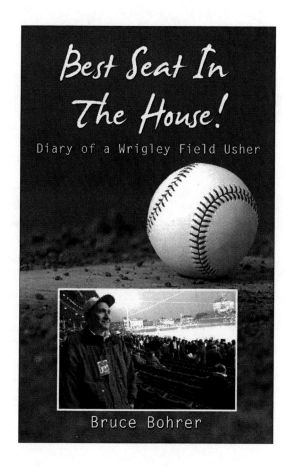

The Best Seat In The House is available at:
www.EckhartzPress.com

**ECKHARTZ
PRESS**